William Tate Groom

**With Havelock from Allahabad to Lucknow, 1857**

William Tate Groom

**With Havelock from Allahabad to Lucknow, 1857**

ISBN/EAN: 9783337219666

Printed in Europe, USA, Canada, Australia, Japan

Cover: Foto ©ninafisch / pixelio.de

More available books at **www.hansebooks.com**

# WITH HAVELOCK

## FROM

## TO

...DON
...ARSTON...
*Limited*
...ston's House
FLEET STREET, E.C.
1894

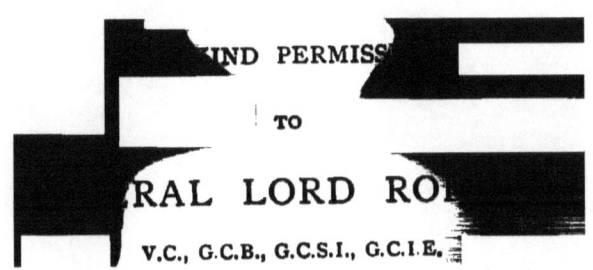

...IND PERMISS...
TO
...RAL LORD RO...
V.C., G.C.B., G.C.S.I., G.C.I.E.

NOTWITHSTANDING that the Indian Mutiny is now an event long past, and the facilities of modern education and travel tend to obliterate quickly the memory of circumstances which, at the time of their occurrence, were of thrilling interest, I venture to publish these extracts from letters which were written to me from day to day by my late dear husband, when he was marching under General Havelock to the relief of Lucknow, feeling sure that there are still many survivors of those days to whom the letters will be interesting ; and I also publish them for the benefit of my grandson, Arthur Forbes Shirreff, and boys of his age, in the hope that whatever be their lot in life, they may endeavour to emulate the heroism of one who, young in years and of a most tender and loving nature, faced hardship, fatigue, and danger with a cheerful courage that never flagged.

Perhaps it is due to those who kindly feel disposed to read these letters, and yet are unacquainted with the leading circumstances under which they were written, to state that my late husband's regiment, the 1st Madras Fusiliers, was one of the oldest in the Honourable East India Company's Service, having fought under Stringer Lawrence, Clive, Coote, Cornwallis and other famous leaders. After the amalgamation of the Honourable East India Company's Service with that of Her Imperial Majesty's Army, the Regiment was known for many years as the 102nd, but it is now called H.M. Royal Dublin Fusiliers. In the year 1857 this Regiment garrisoned Fort

St. George, at Madras; and, because it was composed of Europeans, was sent to Calcutta by Sir Patrick Grant, K.C.B., the then Commander-in-Chief of the Madras Army, in order that it might proceed up country at once, and help to quell the mutiny which was spreading in Bengal.

Their Colonel (afterwards Brigadier-General Neill) distinguished himself at an early period of the campaign, by suppressing the Mutineers of Benares on the 3rd of June.

A part of the corps was amongst the first to arrive at Allahabad, and with some other regiments formed the force over which General Havelock was appointed, and on the 7th July they started on their perilous march, first to Cawnpore, and then to push on to the relief of Lucknow. Fighting their way from day to day, they soon reached and took Cawnpore, and there alas! became aware of the saddest event of those terrible times, viz. the massacre by the insurgents of the European women and children. Anxiety to relieve Lucknow caused General Havelock to hurry forward, and the 22nd and 23rd of July found him with his little army crossing the Ganges into Oude, a small Kingdom which had lately been annexed to British rule. In Oude they fought several battles, but towards the middle of August the General reluctantly felt obliged to retrace his steps to Cawnpore. Cholera as well as fighting had so reduced his numbers that there was no alternative but to wait for reinforcements. These arrived about the 15th September with General Outram in command, and then the recruited column recrossed the river, and began its final advance on Lucknow, which was entered on the 25th. To that memorable day these letters do not extend, owing to the complete interruption of the usual means of conveying intelligence. Lady Inglis, in her interesting book "The Siege of Lucknow," has given a vivid description of the joy with which the army under Generals Havelock and Outram were welcomed by the beleaguered garrison. Thus reinforced they kept the enemy at bay, until adequate relief arrived under the command of Lord Clyde.

This however did not happen until November, and in the interim there was perpetual fighting between the troops in Lucknow and the rebels surrounding them. Valuable lives were lost almost daily. Among them was that of my dear husband, who was mortally wounded in a sortie on the 5th October. While on the march to Lucknow he had heard of the birth of his little daughter, receiving at the same time a tiny lock of her hair, and doubtless the hope of being spared to see her caused him many a pleasant thought in the midst of his anxieties and dangers. But the meeting was not to be. He died in the Residency Hospital, and they buried him in the same spot with many of his comrades, and now violets bloom where these heroes were laid.

HELEN M. I. GROOM.

# INTRODUCTION.

EXTRACTS from letters written to his wife by Lieutenant William Tate Groom, an officer in the 1st Madras Royal Fusiliers. He was born August 10th, 1831. Educated at Rugby School. Entered the Hon. E.I.C. Service in 1850, served in the Burmese war of 1852-1853 (Burmese Medal, Pegu clasp). Was ordered with his regiment to join General Havelock's Force in quelling the Indian Mutiny, May, 1857. Fought all through this campaign until he was wounded, after entering Lucknow, in a sortie on the 5th of October, lingering until the 21st, when he died in the Residency Hospital.

# WITH HAVELOCK

FROM

# ALLAHABAD TO LUCKNOW.

───◆───

Sasseram,
Thirteen miles south of Benares,
On the Grand Trunk Road
*June 8th*, 1857.

I seize the opportunity of an hour or two's rest to write a line to you; perhaps the last you will get for some time, as all communication is stopped north of Benares.

The rebellion has spread all over Bengal and the mutineers are in possession of eleven out of seventeen Treasuries.

We hope to get into Benares to-morrow morning. The night before last, the 37th B.N.I. mutinied in Benares, and were fired into and dispersed by some 200 of *ours* and the 10th Queen's. Some of the Sikhs Regiment were killed by accident, and they went off too; but it is reported that they returned yesterday, and have had 10,000 rupees given them by the head magistrate. Allahabad has revolted. At Ferozpore, Her Majesty's 61st cut one regiment to pieces, and the other corps laid down their arms. The 4th Cavalry stuck to us. A portion of the Gwalior contingent have gone over to the enemy. Punjab ready to rise if any mistake is made at Delhi, which is to be attacked to-day.

I left Calcutta on the night of the 4th June by rail, and we arrived at Raniganj at two o'clock in the morning of the 5th.

Renaud, Stephenson, Grant, Fraser and Spurgin went on in carriages immediately. Seton and I started on the same day at six o'clock in the evening, and ran 100 miles by twelve o'clock noon on the 6th. We dined, and at four o'clock p.m. again started and caught up the others at Sherghatti, where they had stopped by order, on account of the revolt in Benares. We, however, last night got a telegraph despatch, "All clear, come on," so we have run on to this place, and start for Benares at four o'clock p.m. We are all armed with guns, revolvers, etc., and keep a bright look-out. There are Sowars all along the road, so I think we can give a good account of ourselves.

The Ghoorkas have taken Simla, but have not committed any outrages. They allowed the ladies and children to proceed to Dugshai.

No clue yet arrived at as to the cause of the mutiny, but it is generally supposed that the annexation of Oude, Nagpore and Tanjore, and the squashing of the Madras potentate is the real cause of the alarm. They also fancy that Lord Canning was purposely sent out to make them all Christians. All these things, together with the new cartridge alarm too, have caused the revolt.

They say that all the ladies in Benares are in the Mint with a strong guard over them. At Cawnpore, they are in an entrenched barrack. At Lucknow, in the Residency. At Agra, in the fort. Lots of ladies are in a little fort at Chunar, and we have sent twenty-five of our men to take care of them. I suppose a stronger force will be sent out directly it can be spared, and they will be brought into Benares. I do not think the rebels can do much more mischief *now*, *below* Benares, as troops are pouring up the Grand Trunk Road, and also by the steamer on the Ganges. The mischief they can do *above* is awful to think of. I am very glad General Sir Patrick Grant has been sent for, and hope to see him in Benares before the end of the month.

Colonel Neill is acting brigadier.

---

Allahabad, *June* 14*th*, 1857.

You have doubtless heard of all the horrors that have been perpetrated, so I need not recount them.

I reached Benares safely, and was sent off the same night, with 100 men, Stephenson, and Bailey to reinforce the garrison at Allahabad.

After three nights' march through a country in a state not to be described, (villages and towns all in flames, and the shrieks of the unfortunate villagers being plainly heard all along the road) we reached the banks of the Ganges on the 12th. We were surrounded the whole way, but the wretches never came within shot, and were merely looking out for plunder. Such work I never had in my life, and I am only just now able to sit up, and feel a little life in me again, after the exposure to the sun and want of rest.

We are surrounded here by sepoys, mussulmen, villagers, and in fact all mankind. Food very short, and our men are dying in an awful way from overwork and exposure.

We found a wing of a Sikh Corps in garrison here, and Neill got them out last night to the great relief of everybody. We now breathe in peace.

The enemy are in a very strong position

in a place called "The King's Garden," three miles off nearly. We fire round shot perpetually at his outposts, and to-day we are going to try two huge mortars, and see if we can't touch him up a bit.

No news from Delhi and Cawnpore; in fact the whole country north of Benares is in the hands of the rebels. Sad work! and no one knows how or when it will end. I shall, I hope, keep well. To-day is the first day my head has been itself, and I am on main guard.

Our men behaved nobly at Benares the other day. They (30) covered the guns, and H.M. 10th (200) as they advanced on the 37th B.N.I. and Sikh regiments.

Our rifles are the admiration of everybody, and we astonish the niggers not a little.

*Same day.*

Allahabad, *June* 14*th*, 1857.

I wrote you a long letter this morning, and sent it to the Brigadier (Colonel Neill), in order to insure its being sent by a river steamer that leaves for Calcutta to-night with a large number of ladies and children who have been saved (it has never reached him). I arrived in Benares on the 9th of June, and the same night we (Stephenson, Bailey and 100 men) started for this place, and by God's blessing reached it in safety.

The whole country is in arms, and the few native servants left in the fort seem to be going off rapidly.

We are quite safe here, with some 250 of ours, 150 volunteers (railway folk, etc., and about thirty invalid artillery). We have lots of food (of a kind) and plenty of ammunition and water.

I am in a great state of anxiety about you all in Madras. We never get any news save by reports, which of course cannot be relied on. I cannot give you any news from here, as I cannot tell into whose hands this letter may fall. The letter I wrote this morning has evidently been stolen by the native to whom I gave it. He will not find anything to encourage either himself or friends. The horrors going on in Bengal are enough to appal the stoutest hearts. Such a scene of desolation as the whole country presents would not be believed on paper.

---

Allahabad, 26*th June*, 1857.

All well up to this. The cholera has stopped almost entirely. One of our men yesterday, and none to-day as yet.

Renaud has just come in from Benares, he says 800 men are there, chiefly 78th and 64th. All coming on as fast as possible. Colonel Havelock is coming here as Brigadier General to command; and we shall have four European regiments and two or three batteries of artillery in a week or two. I fancy we shall then begin on our own account. We have lots of officers attached to us. Worth, H.M. 60th, Lieutenant Moorsom, 52nd, Morland and Hall, 1st Bengal Infantry, Pearson, 54th B.N.I., Captain Barrow of *our* cavalry is also with us. Swanston of our 7th is with the Sikhs. We have had no fighting since I last wrote. Intelligence has been received of the fall of Delhi, and the capture of the king, who is to be hanged!!! Hurrah!!! All officers are quite well. The dawks now come in daily from Calcutta, so I hope you will get a line every day from me. Colonel Neill has had such a letter from Sir Patrick Grant, thanking the regiment, which he calls "his dear lambs," for the work they have done.

---

Allahabad, *June* 29*th*, 1857.

All well up to this. Some more men of the 84th came in yesterday, also a company of the 64th.

General Havelock comes in to-morrow morning, his staff the day after. He sent in an order to have two full regiments, and six guns ready to advance to the relief of Cawnpore by the end of the week.

The Sikhs (who always appear to get the very best intelligence) heard last night, that General Wheeler was doing well at Cawnpore, and though surrounded, he was able to make sallies now and then, and inflict sufficient punishment to keep the insurgents at a respectful distance. Sir Henry Lawrence is holding his ground well at Lucknow, but there is a strong force round him. The whole of Oude is lost save Lucknow, and it will be smart work if we save that. Poor Sir Henry is very dangerously ill, they say, and should anything happen to him, I fear that Lucknow would fall. We expect Grant, Dale and our men from Ghaziepore to-night, and 300 of the 64th in the *Mirzapore*, and coal steamers. This was once a lovely place (three weeks ago). The cantonments are magnificent, such fine roads, and grand old trees on each side of them, so that at mid-day one could drive about from house to house in the shade. Some of the houses must also have been very fine, all save three or four now occupied by troops have been completely destroyed. The church, a large and very handsome building, is now occupied by troops. The rebels completely smashed all the pews, the altar, ceiling, and painting, and tore every Bible and prayer-book they could find into little shreds.

We hear that everyone is in great alarm in Bangalore, guns in all the barracks, and troops parading for church armed. It is a very wise precaution, for the mutiny here has most effectually proved how little we know of sepoys or any natives. Yesterday (Sunday) I was on a court martial, trying a native, who after a most lengthy and elaborate investigation, turned out to be one of the only men who can be trusted about here. He had pointed out the houses of several Budmashes in the city, and the Shiristadar[1] and head of police trumped up two false charges against him to get him out

[1] The head native official of a law court.

of the way; they being a pair of the greatest scoundrels in the place. I have just found out that no postage stamps are to be got here, so you will have to pay one anna for my letters. I have got one rupee and three annas, and Major Stephenson owes me fifteen rupees!!! so I am quite rich. I don't know what we shall do for want of money. The men have had no pay this month at all.

We have had a magnificent fall of rain which has laid the dust and cleaned out the drains of the fort. We all feel very smart and fresh after it. Cholera nearly entirely disappeared, and a little pay, and 2000 pair of boots, and a few spare boxes of rifle ammunition would do wonders for us. Fancy! We are armed with rifles and have hardly any cartridges left. There are none in any arsenal in Bengal save at Calcutta.

Allahabad, *July 3rd*, 1857.

This will be the last letter that you must expect for some time. We advance to-morrow morning, at least that is the order, and after quitting this, we plunge into utter anarchy and desolation. No post-offices! No meat! No drink! no nothing! I was on main guard yesterday, and at 2 o'clock a.m. had to open the gate for an officer who had come in with dispatches from Renaud, forty miles ahead. He says they have received intelligence in camp, of the fall of Cawnpore, and the massacre of the whole of the Europeans there. A Rajah told Sir Hugh Wheeler that if he would quit the place at once, they might do so without molestation by boats. He, being very short of food, listened to the fiend, who got 120 boats for the party who embarked, and pushed off; no sooner were they in the river, than he opened fire on them from his heavy guns, and killed large numbers. Many jumped from the boats and reached the opposite shore, but were immediately cut to pieces by a body of 2000 cavalry, who have been patrolling the road to keep out all communication between Cawnpore and Lucknow.

He told me all this, and then galloped straight to the general's tent. Shortly after lights flickered there, and great has been the consternation all the morning.

This morning orders show Stephenson, Grant, myself, Dangerfield and Seton with 200 men to Cawnpore to-morrow; with us, 64th, 84th, and I hope some guns. Thirty of the R.A. have just arrived. Renaud's party I believe have been ordered to halt, and await our arrival, as the enemy must now be in great force on the road, and 400 men cannot possibly take Futtehpore—1400 will be better able to manage it. Græme and Hornsby are both in Calcutta, I see, and will doubtless very shortly join us. Spurgin and Arnold went in the steamer with 100 men this morning. I do not think they will reach Cawnpore as the river is falling very rapidly. I shall keep this open till five o'clock (it is now about one p.m.), and will let you know the last news and orders.

---

*5.30 p.m.*

I do not think we can possibly start to-morrow, I see no chance of our getting carriage. We may move into camp. Some alterations have taken place since the morning.

We shall start thus—

|        |     |     |
|--------|-----|-----|
| H.M. 64th | ... ... | 684 |
| H.M. 78th | ... ... | 223 |
| 1st M.F.  | ... ... | 200 |
| Artillery | ... ... | 30  |

Total 1137 Europeans

and 130 Sikhs.

We shall have also six guns with us, I hope, and when we catch up Renaud, we shall have nearly 1600 fighting men, with eight guns. We *ought* to give these gentlemen a dressing! I sincerely hope we may.

---

Camp, Allahabad, *July 5th*, 1857.

We moved into camp last night, and I believe we march to-morrow morning at one o'clock. Early rising, is it not? I fancy we shall be on our legs till twelve or one to-morrow, and perhaps not have the baggage up then. We are encamped on the glacis of the fort, and it is very comfortable *now* as I have a chair, table and cot; but all these superfluous luxuries I shall have to leave behind.

One small hackery for our tent and baggage is all that is allowed. Poor Sir Charles Napier would have been charmed, I am sure, at the scantiness of our apparel, etc.

No news from anywhere this morning, but we very much fear that Cawnpore must have fallen after all, as we have no news from Sir Hugh of any kind. However, it is impossible to say, as the whole country between Futtehpore and Cawnpore is in the hands of the enemy.

---

*Later in the day.*

We have just received more news from

Renaud. He says, "A man has just arrived from Cawnpore and has stated that seven days ago the Rajah withdrew his men, and that Sir H. Wheeler immediately left his entrenchments, hoisted the English flag in the bazaar, and is now in full possession of the place!!" I think that *this* story is more likely than the horrible account brought in two days ago. We have not marched yet, still short of provisions. Our camp makes a very grand front. It looks as if three whole regiments were on the ground, and two batteries of artillery. I suppose this is a dodge of the General's to impress the natives with a wholesome awe of the forces.

If Cawnpore is clear, we shall march on Lucknow, and relieve Sir H. Lawrence, who must be looking very anxiously for support. All the ladies have been ordered out of this place, and Benares, in case of any fresh row; and many left this morning in a river steamer for Calcutta.

I must wind up as the General threatens to move. Grant and I march with a very small sepoy tent between us—no mess tent or anything. I am quite well and strong now, after the rest here.

---

Allahabad, *Tuesday, July 7th*, 1857.

One line from me; we start at two o'clock this afternoon. Yesterday the rain poured in torrents the whole day, and our camp was one huge swamp, all our things wet, and I was unable to find a place to write you a line on. Cawnpore has fallen; I am sorry to say under circumstances of awful atrocity. All the men are in high spirits, and are not as yet affected by the exposure, but I fear we must have a great deal of sickness ere long. A fight at Benares yesterday, 800 of the enemy killed, none of ours hurt. I must stop short as I have not a minute. We are just parading to discharge rifles.

Rain coming up now; we shall have a wet march, I don't expect to be *dry* again for a long time.

---

Camp Koh, 9*th July*, 1857.

I just write a hurried line to say that we are all well up to this. On the evening of the 7th, we left Allahabad in one of the heaviest showers of rain I ever was in. Our own band played us out. The Highlanders had their pipes (five), which seemed to astonish the niggers not a little. We went seven miles that night, and were encamped in a swamp!! Next morning, to everybody's delight, we moved on six miles to better ground, and this morning we have made twenty-seven miles from Allahabad.

Renaud writes this morning, and says that Spurgin was attacked by 500 men and one gun, as he was going up the river. He landed his men, charged the gun, spiked it, and threw it down a well, putting the enemy utterly to flight. He also says that Nana Sahib is coming down the road to meet us. He is probably not aware that he has to meet 1500 Europeans with eight guns. I only hope he will not find out his mistake and return without the pleasure of an interview. He must be caught somehow or other. His atrocities no one can describe.

I have not heard any news except that all the Sikhs that mutinied at Benares have been cut to pieces by the Oude people, who seem to hate them as much as they do us. This little incident will, I think, most effectually put a stop to any more Sikhs defecting in that part of the world, at all events. I feel pretty well again, but get very tired from marching. I have no horse or pony, and thirteen miles is rather a long walk before breakfast. I shall soon get into the swing of it though, and shall not feel it then at all. If more troops are sent rapidly from England, we ought very soon to settle these villains and get the country quiet again, and I suppose that then we may have a chance of getting home.

Everyone here seems to think that the Company's rule is over now; and that Government will, immediately on the receipt of the intelligence of the mutiny and rebellion, advise Her Majesty to rule India herself. I quite think so.

I shall, I hope, be able to write again to-morrow, but am not sure; this will be sent in through the General's people.

---

Camp, *July* 11*th*, 1857.

We reached this ground, name unknown, at nine a.m., after walking seventeen miles! Lots of men in hospital of course; but the General could not help it, as Renaud, five miles in our front, sent in intelligence last night of the very greatest importance from Lucknow. Sir Henry Lawrence has been attacked, lost one of his forts and four guns. He must also have lost a large quantity of provisions, as he says it will be all over by the 20th. God help him! I do not think we can possibly relieve him by that time, as we shall have every inch of ground disputed from Futtehpore to

Cawnpore and Lucknow. We have no cavalry except 150 Sowars, that we cannot depend upon. I am pretty well, only rather tired from the long marches that we are obliged to take. I shall finish this to-morrow. Good-night.

*12th, 5 p.m.*

We had our first fight this morning at eight a.m., and by one it was over. Eleven guns taken, and Futtehpore in our hands! The General is of course delighted! Now I must tell you all about it. After our awful walk yesterday, we were all not a little astonished to find that we were to march again at eleven that night : distance eighteen miles. We groaned when our bugles sounded the rouse, and the pipes of the Highlanders began "Hey Johnnie Cope," however, away we went, and joined

Renaud's force at about two in the morning; at seven o'clock we halted on a plain, with topes and a swamp to the right about a mile off, a rising mound in front about 700 yards distance, and to the left paddy fields, and broken ground. Our artillery was left on the road that ran straight up the centre of our position. The 78th, selves, and cavalry began to pitch our tents on the right, and the 84th, 64th and Sikhs on the left of the road. One hundred of our men were ordered to proceed two miles up the road, and one hundred Sowars four miles (in fact nearly up to Futtehpore), to make a reconnaissance. I was quite done up, and had lain down under a tree to sleep, when Beatson, the Adjutant-General of the force, rode up and told us " that our men were retiring, and that the enemy was advancing in force." Hardly had the words left his mouth, when they opened upon us with their guns at an impossible distance, and large bodies of cavalry were seen moving to our flanks. As their guns came down the road ours opened on them, and at the same time we all formed quarter distance column, and advanced in echelon from the right, covered by our skirmishers. It was a short, sharp and very decisive affair. Our rifles completely upset their cavalry. They fled, leaving all their guns, a large quantity of tents and ammunition, etc., in our hands, eleven guns of kinds 18s, 24s, and 9 and 6 prs. We did not lose a man! Three have died of fatigue, which was to be expected, as we were all in the sun until three o'clock. I fear many more must have died, as they were lying all over the town when the rear guard came through. It has altogether been a very fortunate affair. The sepoys engaged were 1st, 53rd, 6th, Gwalior

Artillery, 2nd Light Cavalry and some irregular regiment. The cavalry all fought in their regimentals; infantry in white clothing.

---

*13th July,* 1857.

We halted here to-day luckily for me. I had a nasty attack of fever last night from over-fatigue, and the rest has been of great service to me. I hope to be all well again to-morrow. I must stop now as it makes my head ache sitting up.

---

Camp Mullipore, sixteen miles from Futtehpore, *July* 14th, 1857.

We left the scene of our first victory at three this morning. I was on the sick list, as I told you in my last letter, and had to come in a dhoolie. I am very much better, and I shall hope to be quite well in time for the storm and sack of Cawnpore, which little event we hope may come off the day after to-morrow. We have heard that the head of the rebels there, is a Mahratta chief, and that all the women and children are safe in his palace at Bithoor. If so, please God, we shall be able to save them. He, of course, has been keeping them as hostages in case of his capture at Cawnpore.

The General has estimated the force we licked on Sunday at 2500. They had arrived at Futtehpore the same morning as ourselves, so their stay there was brief. One hundred Sikhs returned towards Allahabad this morning, to see that the road is kept open. I do not think I told you of our loss on the occasion of the battle of Futtehpore. We lost five men from *coup de soleil*, and the other regiments about five between them. We were skirmishing in the sun up to our knees, and occasionally *waists* in water all the morning. One poor fellow was shot in his tent last night accidentally by a comrade.

Men and officers are tolerably healthy and fresh, considering the work we are all doing, which is anything but light.

On the line of march this morning we found in a village twenty-five casks of porter, *fancy that!* It is the best thing we have done yet. Guns are all over the country, but porter is not.

The guns we captured on Sunday came chiefly from Nowgong—in fact it was the Nowgong company of artillery that was in the field. I must now stop and take a sleep, as we go on at 11 o'clock to night; so good-bye.

I had no idea a week ago that I should have a chance of sending any more letters for a fortnight; mind, you must not be astonished at a sudden stoppage.

---

Camp, 15*th July*, 1857.

We have had two fights this morning, but have of course held our own. The enemy's practice with a twenty-four siege gun, which was planted on a bridge over a wide nullah, was mighty creditable, but very disagreeable. I feel very seedy to-day after it all, so cannot give you a very full account. As usual we were in front, and to-day got rather peppered.

Poor Renaud very badly wounded leading the men into action. I fear he will lose his leg. Fraser a contused wound in the elbow, my pay sergeant is also badly wounded, but none of *us* killed; 78th one killed, other regiments I know nothing about. We have taken four guns to-day. I am very sick of the constant harassing work, it is incessant; and from exposure and fatigue, I really feel very far from serene. I must stop now, it is so late; indeed I only wrote a line in case you might hear of the second skirmish through some other channel.

---

Cawnpore, 17*th July*, 1857.

By God's blessing I am again able to let you know how we are. You must not be astonished at any eccentric grammar or English, for my head is in a whirl from exposure and want of rest. Yesterday morning I was on the sick list from a mild sun-stroke, the effects of the two previous

**D**

days' fighting. We started from our ground at 5 a.m., and intended halting four miles from Cawnpore. After proceeding about eleven miles, one of our scouts came in and informed the General that the enemy had thrown up works commanding the road two miles in our front; he ordered us to bivouac (it was then 9 a.m.), and told us he intended storming the enemy's position and taking Cawnpore that day. He gave us till one o'clock, and then the bugles sounded the assembly.

The whole of the sick and wounded, baggage and commissariat were ordered to remain behind, but I got leave from the doctor to come on in a dhoolie, and when the fight opened I was as fresh as possible, though very weak. I am glad I came on, for I saw as hard a day's fighting as falls to the lot of most soldiers.

Fusiliers in advance of course, and we

showed them how to drive *whole regiments* out of snug positions by a couple of extended companies with Enfield rifles. Their grape and canister told very severely on us; and, horrible to say, the cavalry cut up a very large portion of our wounded and stragglers. After our final advance in line and utter rout of the enemy, we halted, and the General rode down the ground of the 78th and Fusiliers. You never heard anything like the cheering. We slept on our ground that night, with nothing but our swords and muskets for our pillows, and I woke up this morning as filthy and refreshed a man as any in the camp. We moved into the cantonment shortly after daybreak, and our baggage came up about twelve; so I write from a comfortable tent. I am much exhausted, but am decidedly better than I have been since Futtehpore.

Spurgin and the steamer arrived and anchored at eleven this morning, so we shall be able to cross the river to-morrow. The General says he intends going to Lucknow in two days (fifty miles)! He seems quite unconscious that any soldier can ever get fatigued, and accordingly punishes us very unmercifully.

Captain Beatson, his Adjutant-General, is dying, I fear, of cholera, brought on by overwork and exposure. Poor Currie of the 84th, who was commanding the detachment of that regiment, was frightfully wounded yesterday. Stirling, commanding the 64th, was also hit, so now half of the officers commanding have been wounded. We continue to receive the most complimentary messages from Sir Patrick Grant, who calls us "his dear lambs." I fear that "his dear lambs" are rapidly getting exhausted, and we shall want a fresh supply of them. All these warlike tales must not frighten you, only I think it is much better that you should hear all the accounts from me than through the *Athenæum*.

---

Cawnpore (no date).

The day before yesterday, Ours, the Sikhs, the cavalry and two guns went to Bithoor, the nest of the fiend who commanded the insurgents here. We started at 10 a.m., and got there about four. We found that he had fled, and all his following dispersed.

We found twenty guns, the whole of which we brought in yesterday, having bivouacked in the Nana's compound. He had a magnificently furnished English house, with all sort of cows, dogs, horses and sheep, in a large English paddock.

We looted a good deal. One man of

mine (my own servant) got 600 rupees. I have a chair and a silver plate, which I hope I shall be able to keep. We arrived in camp last night, and found General Neill and 200 of the 84th, the Highlanders, and 64th had crossed the river. We expect to get an order to do the same hourly. Poor Renaud died this morning, his leg was amputated yesterday, and he was much better, but he sank suddenly this morning. They say that the insurgents round Lucknow are reduced to firing stones. Sir Henry Lawrence is dead, I fear. You had better address me now, General Havelock's Column, Cawnpore.

---

Cawnpore, *July* 22nd, 1857.

Here we are still, and the rain falling in torrents.

Nearly the whole of the Force are now on the other side of the river without tents. They say that the Sikhs are to cross this morning, and we cross this evening. No tents or baggage to be taken to Lucknow, so you may fancy what a comfortable time we shall have of it. Raikes and a hundred men remain here with some other troops in an entrenched camp under General Neill. We have heard no firing for some time now. I think they must be really getting short of ammunition.

The last camp shave is, " They are all quite comfortable at Lucknow, and can hold out till August."

Still no news from the north. The rebels are in full possession for the present. However, we have made all clear from Cawnpore to Calcutta, which is a good slice of road.

I do not think I told you that the General, after the Battle of Cawnpore, gave ourselves and the 78th a Victoria Cross for the man most worthy of it. When all behaved so well, it was very difficult to find any one man who had distinguished himself above his comrades. But I believe that Colour-Sergeant James Kelly, acting sergeant-major of our detachment, is to have the decoration.

I am sure that the whole regiment will be proud of having such an honourable decoration in its ranks, and I believe that a better soldier than Kelly cannot be found anywhere to carry it. He has been very badly wounded in the hand and arm, but is getting well rapidly. Poor Currie of the 84th died here of his wounds, and Beatson, our Adjutant-General, of cholera; so these officers of the Force have now been buried in front of our camp.

One of the peculiar features of this place is the plague of flies. I had often heard of them, but, if I had not seen it, could not have believed it possible that so many flies existed in the world. You cannot conceive the nuisance they are. I would rather have millions of mosquitoes than suffer the agonies of annoyance caused by the Cawnpore fly.

I got a saddle and bridle here yesterday for twenty rupees.

I am going to send you by Dr. Howell a new dress, a present from Captain Grant, *looted* of course, and a silver tray from myself; that is if Howell goes away, which is not quite certain. He has been unwell for some time, and unfit for work, and as we have two others, Rean and Robertson, with us, I think they might spare him.

One of my men found at Bithoor a pair of thorough bred English bull-dogs, they will bring him 500 rupees at least in Calcutta if he can only manage to keep them. No words can describe the state of mud and filth the camp is in this morning. The rain is still coming down in torrents, and we hourly expect to have to go and bivouac in it on the Oude side of the river.

I had a really good night's rest last night for the first time since I left Allahabad. I do not expect another for the next six months. I must now conclude, as I am getting near an end of my paper.

---

Cawnpore, *July 23rd*, 1857.

Here still. All well. All have now crossed or are crossing the river except ourselves and Sikhs. I suppose we shall be off in an hour or two. I heard yesterday that the rebels had exhausted all their gun ammunition and were firing stones and tent pegs for two days, when they were suddenly stopped, and retired out of range of Sir Henry's guns. No one knows what they are at. I suppose they are making preparations to meet us. Nana Sahib has joined Nana Sing at Lucknow, and the Force that we drove out of Cawnpore are about seventy miles up the Agra road.

The rain is still falling very hard indeed, and we shall have frightful work of it, I fear, in the mud and rain.

*Later.*

We have made a move at last, and have got down to the bank of the river, where we are, men and all, in one house, with the whole of our baggage and horses in the compound, so that you can fancy we are not troubled with much extra dress. I expect we shall cross the river to-morrow; 64th, 84th, and 78th are over, and the artillery are now crossing. We hear that the enemy are making *wondrous* preparations for us in Oude, 16 miles off. There are about 20,000 men in arms now in Oude, but they appear to have no leaders, and I do not think we shall have more than one good fight. We have had a fine morning, but the rain is creeping up again.

---

Camp in Oude, opposite Cawnpore,
*July* 25, 1857.

We crossed the river last night in a pelting shower of rain, and marched up to the General's position, which we reached at dark. As a *special favour* we were allowed to remain on the road ! ! ! Our proper position in the line was knee deep in water, and great was the difficulty Stephenson had in keeping us out of it.

We were hurried up yesterday as the General fancied he might be attacked, and we accordingly bivouacked on the road. Luckily it did not rain, and I found a man of the 60th Rifles who is doing adjutant-general's work who had a cold fowl; he gave me a leg, which, with the biscuit and a ration of rum which each man had served out to him in the dark, afforded me a famous dinner. This morning we fell back half a mile, and are now occupying two little mud villages. I am with Dangerfield and Bailey under a tree, and am quite comfortable. Sir H. Bernard has died of cholera at Delhi, which is still in the hands of the rebels.

Road all clear now from Cawnpore to

Benares. Colonel Wilson of the 64th arrived by carriage dawk this morning.

I fancy Hamilton and Arthur have also arrived in Cawnpore with the band and colours and 30 men. I expect we shall move but a short way to-morrow morning so as to have a shorter march before our first fight in Oude.

---

Bivouac at a village 5 miles from Oude bank of the river,

*26th July*, 1857.

Another line to let you know I am well. We are waiting here for our food, and 170 of our men who are not across the river. Hamilton, Gosling and Arthur will be with us to-night, I expect. The General says he will march to-morrow, whether the men and stores are up or not. The place we are now in is a little better than our last bivouac. It rained, though, last night in torrents. Our cavalry has just gone ahead reconnoitring. The enemy, they say, are in position about ten miles to our front. Lots of reports flying about. I am sorry to say that cholera has made its appearance in the Force, and we have lost a great many men, chiefly 64th and Artillery. *We* had a case or two last night, none yet fatal. We certainly cannot afford to lose a man at this juncture.

I write to you every day and send the letters to the General's tent, then trust to Providence. I hope you get them all, though I can hardly fancy that you can, as so many letters seem to miscarry owing to the continued disturbance in Central India.

General Neill has just captured in a village near Cawnpore the subada-major of the 1st B.N.I., one of the greatest scoundrels loose. He intends making him clean a portion of the house where all the unfortunate women were killed, and then will hang him at the door—that's the way to treat these men.

I saw in the *Athenæum* of the 9th, Colonel Cotton's noble offer of 1000 rupees to head a subscription for relief of sufferers, and I think it does him credit. I wish someone would get up a subscription for officers who have lost all their kits and horses, etc. I am reduced to three flannel shirts, three socks, three handkerchiefs and one shell jacket; two pair of trousers, two pair of shoes, two blankets and a waterproof cover. Where the rest of my property is no one knows. It is scattered about impartially all over Bengal.

Dale and Chisholm are in Cawnpore. They arrived yesterday, and Græme and Hornsby are in Allahabad. The 5th

Fusiliers and 90th have, they say, both left Calcutta for Cawnpore. I wish they were here.

The women in Palaveram all seem to be in a great state of alarm, judging from the letters their husbands get. I hope the Government are taking care of them and looking after them. All the wives of the 64th and 78th get free rations and beer at Bombay, as long as their regiments are away.

We are all in a great state of delight at the prospect of seeing Gosling and Hamilton joining us to-day in white trousers and gorgeous array. If you could only see us, you would stare with wonder at our state of dirt and dishevelment. Flannel shirts, jack boots, and enormous turbans will make Gosling open his eyes with horror. One consolation is, that he must lapse into the same state after one night's rain. Now good-bye.

. Did I tell you what that miscreant Nana Sahib said to his army after the battle of Oonao? "Kill all the men in dirty shirts and blue caps, they kill all my men before they fire." I am very glad we made such an impression on him. We wounded his brother at Futtipore, and he died four days after.

---

Busharut Gunge, Oude,
*30th July*, 1857.

I could not write to you yesterday, as we were literally fighting from morning till night. We got under arms at four o'clock in the morning, and marched at five; before six we were under fire, and by 9.30 we drove the enemy off the field, having captured fifteen guns. They were as usual very strong in numbers, and in a very good position. They fought much better than the sepoys on the other side of the river.

Poor Richardson was killed, and Seton very badly wounded. I fear the casualty roll of the Force must be very heavy. We marched at two o'clock, and found our friends in a very strong village with five guns, with which they fought right well. We lost a great many in wounded here, and it was past seven o'clock when we got through the village, and bivouacked on the Lucknow side of it. The name of the place where we had our first battle is Oonao, the second took place at Busharut Gunge where we are now. I suppose we shall advance this afternoon. The heat yesterday was fearful. I was exposed to the sun the whole day, and I feel as if all my bones were dried up. My hand is so stiff I can hardly write. I forgot to tell you we took four or five guns here, so we have taken nearly one third of the enemy's guns already.

The General says that he intends making "A splendid" report of the regiment for the way in which we skirmished in the morning and evening. Very gratifying, but we all begin to wish that a small share of the work might be given the 64th and 84th. The 78th and ourselves had it all our own way as usual yesterday, and the fatigue of four or five hours, skirmishing knee deep in mud and water with a Bengal July sun overhead is not small. The enemy's cavalry as usual did nothing. They seem regular hounds. I had several narrow escapes yesterday, but by God's mercy was spared all harm. We shall in all probability have one fight to-morrow or to-night, and an awful scrimmage at Lucknow, of course, and then I hope we may return to Cawnpore.

We have lost 200 men since we have been in Bengal, and we can only muster about 200 men in the field at Head Quarters.

The rest are all sick and scattered. Of course we have more men in camp, but we certainly only go into action 200 strong.

I think it very possible that this letter may not reach you, as the road can hardly be as open from here to Cawnpore as it is below.

---

Camp, seven miles from Cawnpore,
*July* 31*st*.

A hurried line to tell you that we have fallen back about ten miles to this place, name (to me) unknown, and here, from the preparations, we seem likely to stop. No one knows the reason, but it is pretty generally supposed that our Force is totally unfit to advance. We lost killed and wounded on the 29th, between seventy and eighty men. I think it probable that we are awaiting reinforcements. I fancy we shall be off again before long, as troops *must* be coming up.

---

Camp, seven miles from Ganges, Oude,
*August 1st*, 1857.

I wrote you a very short letter yesterday, and put off writing until I was nearly too late altogether for the post. I had not very much to tell you, as it was a very uneventful day, not a shot fired from morning till night. What to-day may bring forth I know not, but we cannot expect to remain here very long without being attacked. From the various preparations being made I think it very possible that the General intends remaining here in position several days. Maycock, of H.M. 53rd, who is one of our D.A. quarter-master generals of the force, told us this morning that he believed that we were to wait here for reinforcements. Where they are to come from (within a fortnight) I cannot conceive, and by that time we shall be hemmed in here, as they are at Lucknow. They will not of course do us very much damage, but it is very disagreeable being penned up like sheep. We have pickets out all round our position of course, and these will give us timely warning of any advance in force.

Grant, Dangerfield, Arnold, self and Bailey are all in a native mud hut. You never saw such a queer little hole in your life. If it was not for the heat and myriads of flies, we should be *almost* comfortable. All the men are either in huts of the same kind, or living under bowers made of branches of trees, and under trees which are thick enough to keep out the sun. Hamilton has collapsed from the exposure to heat and night air, and is laid up with fever and pains in his bones. I was much the same yesterday, but am better to-day. The Major and Frazer both far from well, and indeed all ailing more or less. The General is very much pleased with the Regiment, and told the Major yesterday, that, "Often as he had cause to be pleased with us, he was astonished at the energy and daring displayed by the blue caps on the 29th, and that although he had already had the pleasure of bringing the Regiment to the notice of the G.G., he now intended making a special report of the service rendered by the Regiment on that day." The adjutants of the 84th were both badly wounded on the 29th, and I fear that several officers who have been wounded are very badly so. I think it is the General's intention to send all the wounded and sick into Cawnpore to-night. I am sure I hope they may be sent, as they are far from being comfortable here, poor fellows.

I have just read Major Stephenson's dispatch to the adjutant-general, and am happy to say that he has mentioned my name with Grant and Fraser, and Arnold. It was our luck to be with the skirmishers in the morning, and Dangerfield and Hargood had them in the evening.

I was with the left support in the evening, and with Major Stephenson and Captain Grant got peppered very fairly from the loop-holed houses that covered the enemy's guns and entrance to the village of Busharut Gunge.

3 p.m. We are still quite quiet, but cannot expect to be so much longer. Cawnpore quiet, but hourly expect to be

attacked by the Gwalior and Futtehghar rebels who are making preparations for moving on the place. Seton still doing well, but very much disfigured, poor boy. I hope you get all my wonderful letters. I write every day nearly, under trees, and in tents and all sorts of eccentric places. I am writing this in front of our hut, with three fellows smoking and talking outside all round me, and I write away as snugly and unconcerned as if I were in a gorgeous and quiet library. As I write to my own Nell, I feel my mind quite abstracted from all other matters, and nothing under a heavy gun would rouse me.

---

Camp seven miles from Ganges, Oude,
*August 2nd*, 1857.

Here we are still in our old place, entrenching ourselves and making ourselves as strong as we can to resist the enemy, who are going to make us all into curry directly. I am in great hopes that they will attack us here, as they will most certainly lose more men in the attempt than they ever have done yet. From the preparations being made here, I think it likely that we shall stop for some time in this charming spot.

To-day, Sunday, we were to have paraded for Divine Service at 5.30 a.m., instead of which the enemy's cavalry disturbed one of our cavalry pickets last night, and we turned out at one o'clock and laid down under arms till daylight. My poor bones feel as sore as ever again from exposure. I had no blanket, cloak, or anything. I was rather better yesterday, having slept in a mud hut that I told you of.

Camp Mungulwar, Oude,
*3rd August*, 1857.

We still remain at this village, and have not yet been attacked from any quarter.

We are still in the dark about the General's intentions. Everybody is frightfully disgusted at his conduct; but he doubtless is acting on the best information, and has very good reasons for his apparent want of energy. News came into camp this morning from Delhi. What it is no one knows. The General only deigns to say "It is good," which I suppose means that we have not been actually yet obliged to raise the siege. I wonder when they will storm the place; nearly two months have now elapsed since the siege commenced.

I see by the Madras papers that a subscription has been undertaken for the relief of the families of the regiment. Poor creatures! I am sure they will need it. We have now lost hard on 200 men, and many of them were married.

We are now blessed with wonderfully fine weather, which is a great mercy. I fear we should suffer fearfully if it was to rain. We bury a man every day as it is. How thankful we shall all be to get back to Madras; the work is awful for all ranks—nothing but utter misery and discomfort for the men. I dare not hope to be relieved until we are reduced to the very lowest ebb, and then I suppose the few of us that remain will bring the colours of the regiment back to its Presidency. I hear the 60th Rifles are to go to Madras, which will lessen our chance of return not a little. However, it can't be helped. I hope I may get back some day.

Camp as before, *August 4th*, 1857.

I shall write from the place we have fallen back on, but hear orders have been issued for us to hold ourselves in readiness to march to-morrow morning. Three guns, a few artillerymen, and sixty of the 84th came into camp this morning. I suppose that this is the detachment for which we have been detained. The news from Delhi that arrived yesterday has not leaked out. I fancy it was nothing very wonderful after all.

---

*August 6th*, 1857.

I was stopped the day before yesterday by the bugles sounding the assembly. We had to march to meet the enemy at Busharut Gunge, from which place we had driven him on the 29th. We slept at our arms at a place about four miles from the enemy's position, and yesterday morning went at him and gave him the best licking he has had yet, but we could not take his guns.  They were all horsed. The enemy was so numerous that we were twice completely surrounded, and our rear guard threatened, so we had again to beat a retreat to our old position.

The General yesterday divided his force into three divisions : and we found ourselves taken from the Highlanders and brigaded with the 64th. We were the rear division, but at last we got an order to move to the right flank, and cover three guns that had been sent round to harass the enemy as they crossed the bridge on the other side of the town.

We lined the edge of the water and kept up a jolly fire for a long time, wondering when the bridge was to be taken.  At last we heard a cheer, and the 84th dashed over it with four guns, but they did not seem to get any further, and the bridge being now crowded with guns and limbers, etc., the enemy opened from the front.

Then was the cry, "Where are the Fusiliers?" and away we went some distance back to get on to the road, and threaded our way through the mass which choked the bridge, and supported by the Highlanders, cleared the village in a crack. As we were forming on the other side ready to make a rush, Havelock said, "Hurrah! blue bonnets, that's right, show 'em the way," and we did show them the way in style.

But the day's work was awful, three hours' fighting and twenty miles march. We got back at about 8.30 p.m., and horror! I found I was for an outlying picket. I got some food at 10 p.m., and rolled in a cloak had a jolly sleep. I write this from the picket, from which I shall not be relieved till 5.30 this evening. Pleasant! but unavoidable. There was a report last night that we were to recross the river and await the arrival of a larger force, but staff officers have been all round the place this morning looking for positions for guns, so I fancy we are going to remain here.

We hear that the rebels have raised the siege of Lucknow, and are coming down to exchange compliments with us by way of a change. It is impossible to say what they really intend doing. I have no doubt we must have done the garrison at Lucknow a deal of good by drawing off men and guns from around them, and I trust that they have been enabled to procure more provisions; as long as they have food, they can hold out for ever. Would that all this were over. I am truly tired of this constant marching and countermarching without even tents. We went into action yesterday morning in one of the heaviest downpours of rain I ever remember, and then were baked on an open plain for the rest of the day. Poor old Fusiliers! I wish some of the good folks could see how cheerfully and nobly the "old lambs" bear up against all kinds of fatigue and privations.

---

Camp Mungulwar, Oude.
*7th August*, 1857.

We now hear that we are to return to Cawnpore for certain. It will take some time getting the commissariat across the river again, and then we shall have to embark with the guns, etc. I suppose it will take at least a week before we are all across. We had an alarm last night and were turned out. A few of the enemy's cavalry and infantry came down upon the picket, from which I had just been relieved by Arnold. They all retired on the sentry firing on them.

It is very wet to-day, and we all have to sit crowded in our little hut, and from the heat and flies are all half mad.

---

Mungulwar, Oude, *August 8th*, 1857.

I have not much to tell you to-day, but as usual thankfully greet the chance of being able to write to you. I actually spent a cheerful evening yesterday. We had a wonderful stew made of mutton and potatoes!!! and we got some beer from Cawnpore!! and we all *nearly* got happy, and as we were not turned out during the night, we paraded at reveillé this morning in lighter states of mind than usual.

It rained yesterday incessantly, but to-day we have a lovely sky, and so we are drying all our blankets and clothes, ready for a move in any direction. Out of our small force we have forty in hospital, but I am happy to say only one or two serious cases. Report says this morning that we are again to advance; no one knows the General's intentions. I think that he is very wise in keeping his own counsel, at the same time it is very disagreeable living in this nasty hole in a state of uncertainty as to our future movements.

You will have heard ere this of the mutiny at Dinapore, and the fearful massacre of 150 men and five officers of the 10th N.I., and 37th N.I. at Arrah. It is supposed that those who escaped from the trap into which they were led, have been by this time starved or cut to pieces. They consisted of another hundred gallant men.

Fearful times these! I am most thankful to think that you have all hitherto been spared any of these horrors in Madras.

The inhabitants of Calcutta are all in a fearful state of terror, and all the troops that ought to be with us are detained to take care of the Calcutta folk, who, I should think, with the assistance of the thousands of sailors who are procurable at a minute's notice from the shipping in the Hooghly, ought to be well enough able to take care of themselves.

---

Camp, *9th August*, 1857.

I find that, after all, the chances are in favour of our returning to Cawnpore. I know that the Engineers were employed at the Ghat yesterday morning making a flying bridge, and that boats were employed all day passing bullocks, commissariat, stores, etc., and carts over to the entrenched camp. I believe that very good news has been received from Lucknow, to the effect that they have lots of provisions, ammunition, etc., and feel themselves secure.

We must have drawn off a very large portion of the enemy in our direction, and as the Ghoorkas must have entered Oude by this time, I have no doubt that they are enjoying a few days' quiet and are able to refit and lay in fresh supplies.

The steamer went up the river yesterday to disperse the 42nd B.N.I. Regiment, which has halted a few miles above Bithoor on the bank of the river, and round whom a large number of Budmashes are collecting. We also hear that a large rabble are gathering about twenty miles from Cawnpore, on the Agra Road, with six guns of sorts; so we shall have some work to do if we do recross the river.

I hear that a terrible revenge has been taken on the mutineers at Arrah, for the slaughter that I told you of yesterday.

I am getting quite dissipated! I dined yesterday with the Artillery for the purpose of eating pancakes, and I dine with the Highlanders to-night; so you see we are keeping up our spirits, though we are in Oude and the enemy in our front.

We have, I deeply regret to say, just lost our sergeant-major from cholera, a man whose loss to the regiment is irreparable. He leaves a wife and three children at Palaveram. Do you think you could manage to see her and speak a few words of consolation to the poor woman? The whole regiment attend his funeral this afternoon. Our last date from Madras is the 25th, and I see that folk are subscribing very handsomely for the bereaved families of the Fusiliers.

Camp Mungulwar, Oude.
*August* 10*th*, 1857, 5 *p.m.*

I fear that this letter will not be in time for to-day's dawk, but I have been in a state of preparation for moving since 7 p.m. yesterday.

Last night I went to dine with the Highlanders. Just as I sat down to dinner an orderly came to inform me that my company was to march immediately. Part of 300 men and two guns that were to go off on a secret expedition with one day's food. I swallowed my dinner and rushed home, packed up my bed, and anxiously waited for the order to move. At nine we were told that the movement was postponed until further orders. At nine this morning I was informed that I was on duty, and that the whole force was to move somewhere at 10 a.m. I was to remain behind with twenty men and thirty-five sick, the whole of the bedding and ammunition.

Willis of the 84th (now commanding that corps), as field officer of the day, was sent for by the General, and told that after the departure of the force he was responsible for the position and baggage. He had the guards and pickets, about 200 men, and six guns. We made our arrangements accordingly, and at 10 a.m. the army fell in and remained under arms until 12, when orders came down that the expedition was postponed until further orders. At 4 p.m. I was again informed that I was to be prepared to move off at half an hour's notice with 100 of our men, and 100 of the 84th to go with us. Where we are to go to, no one knows. I have unpacked my bed, and write you this line on the chance of catching the dawk.

Camp Mungulwar, Oude.
11th August, 1857.

As we were going to bed last night, an order came that we were to be ready to march this morning to the front with one day's rations. However, we turned out at reveillé as usual, and the General sounded the retreat, or rather the disperse, a few minutes after sunrise. He had again changed his mind. I hear that the heavy guns leave for the river at 8 p.m. in order that they may reach the Ghat by moonrise, and that the rest of us are to move off at midnight. If he gets us all across safely he will be wonderfully lucky. Report also says we are to go to Agra. I don't exactly see how we can possibly manage that. We have forty sick on this side of the river alone. How they are to be got down is a mystery.

The rebels are awfully in want of caps for their muskets. They say they have taken the nipples off many of their pieces and fire them like matchlocks with a slow match. Caps sell in Delhi for anything, owing to the dawk being cut off at Sasseram. We got no Calcutta news yesterday; Neill had a copy despatch from Delhi "doing well;" only 2000 Europeans left in camp though, cholera has thinned their ranks fearfully.

I don't think I told you that Dale went up the river two or three days ago with fifty men and some guns, and had a fight with 42nd B.N.I. He had three of his men wounded, and they returned the day before yesterday. I do not know what damage he did to the enemy. I do not think that you will hear from me again from this side of the river, at least I hope not. God grant that I may reach Cawnpore safely, and that I may be able to give you good news from there.

---

Entrenched Camp, Cawnpore.
*18th August*, 1857.

I have been unable to write to you for several days for the following reasons. The General made us send everything we had across the river, and at 10 a.m. on the 11th he sent staff officers all over the place to see that nothing was left. Having satisfied himself that not a box of lucifers was in camp, he immediately ordered the column to advance. We marched that afternoon seven miles, and bivouacked in a plain. I had a cloak, luckily—few men had that. It rained too in the night. Next morning we fought another battle and took two guns and lots of horses. Grant was wounded slightly in the leg. That night we returned to our old position, and next morning we went down to the river. Our regiment and the pickets of the night before, with four guns, composed the embarkation crossers, and we were lying in the sand without a rag or mat over us till two o'clock p.m. We were then allowed to move into some huts near the Ghat, and we eventually got into some houses in Cawnpore at nine p.m. You may fancy the luxury of a hasty toilet and a night's rest. I was too tired to eat, and next morning I found I had fever, and I have been laid up ever since, but am very much better to-day. The force went to Bithoor yesterday to turn out the 42nd B.N.I., the 2nd Cavalry, and some Oude Regiment that has occupied the place. Fusiliers had seven killed and five wounded; 78th thirteen wounded, and one officer. It was a sharp affair.

Cawnpore, *August* 19*th*, 1857.

Our little force wonderfully reduced. The last battle at Bithoor was fought by less than 600 Europeans, though four regiments were in the field. Poor Chisholm died last night of cholera, he was taken ill on picket. Campbell of the Highlanders died the night before.

I am very much better to-day, no fever, and shall report well to-morrow.

The other bank of the river swarms with the enemy, who are up to some mischief or other, we can't make out what. The steamer and 100 men under Arnold went twenty miles down the river this morning to put a stop to the proceedings at a town in that direction. They are trying to cross, and as we have a large force, and guns on the Agra Road, and the 42nd B.N.I., and others near Bithoor, 3000 men at

Sharazpore with guns, and some 8000 of Scindiah's troops to keep in check until the Governor-General vouchsafes to send a few men to our aid, we had rather the Oude men kept on their own side of the river. One of the Madras regiments is to go to Benares, and the other to Dinapore.

I don't know what other troops have arrived in Calcutta.

There seems to be great excitement at home about the mutiny, but people know nothing of it yet; every mail carries home new horrors, and when the Cawnpore massacre becomes known I don't know what people will do.

Fifty thousand rupees has been offered now for Nana Sahib. We caught his wife and mother-in-law the other day, but they are of no use. I suppose he will be caught some day, and I hope Neill may have the chance of punishing him. He has devised a punishment for him, I know.

We have a fearful number in hospital, and seventy men, who are too much exhausted to do anything, live in the theatre with a surgeon to look after them. They are called "the invalids," but the whole force might be classed in the same category. Such a lot of woe-begone ragged, bearded ruffians you never saw! Gosling is laid up with fever now. Please God some of us will live through it all. Many can't expect it among the men, for they are really disappearing at a frightful rate.

---

Cawnpore, *August 20th*, 1857.

I write my daily letter as usual, but have not much to tell you. General Outram is appointed to command here, and we hope to see him as soon as he has got Dinapore in order. There is a report to-day that 600 men are coming up from Allahabad, but I fear that the news is too good to be true. The dawk comes in now regularly again, so I suppose the mutineers at Arrah have been dispersed, and the Grand Trunk Road cleared of them for the present.

The camp which has been entrenched near the river, where all the sick live, and all our food and ammunition is stored, is to be abandoned, and a new position taken up. The reason is, that we expect the enemy will shortly commence to fire into it from the other bank of the river. I move from it to-night, and go to our own camp, being reported well. I hear that we have 370 men in the field hospital this morning, so I fancy that the men are improving a little in health. It is, however, a fearful number! No news from the north, and we are pretty quiet this morning as yet. The steamer has not returned from her trip down the river.

Allahabad is to be garrisoned by a naval Brigade of 300 blue-jackets, under the celebrated Captain Peel, who commanded the Naval Brigade in the Crimea.

---

Cawnpore, *August* 21st, 1857.

A very hurried line to-day. I am very busy. I moved into the camp last night from the sick tents, and found them pitched in a delightful swamp, and all at an early dinner which my sort rejected. I am now acting adjutant, and have my hands full of work of all sorts and kinds. I have only just got a moment to write this line to you, as I don't like to let a day go without writing a scrap. No news of any kind from north or south: We stop here at all events for some days, and the men are living in the old Cavalry stables ! ! ! Poor Raikes has had cholera, but is better.

---

Cawnpore, *August* 22nd, 1857.

I moved this morning from our tent down to a corner of the Cavalry stables, where with Hamilton I am located in one of the most decided smells I have ever experienced. Captain Maycock (one of the numerous Dep: Ass. Q.M.G.'s attached to our Force) was here just now, and congratulated me on being so comfortable, and also said that we had cleaned out our stable better than any other Regiment. What a jolly state *they* must be in ! Two officers died last night : Grant, of our 3rd Europeans, who was adjutant of the Volunteer Cavalry, and an officer named Brown, who had escaped the massacre at this station. Three men of the 84th and two of the 64th also died. I am happy to say none of ours taken ill, and Tom Raikes is much better to-day. Frazer and Grant still seedy. Grant's wound is going on very well, and Seton's too. Gosling hopes to be able to go out of camp to-morrow. All the sick and wounded are to be sent to Allahabad as soon as arrangements can be made for sending so large a number of men. We had a highly complimentary order from Sir Colin Campbell last night by electric telegraph, which is now open from here to Calcutta.

We have very nasty weather, and a cold chilly wind blows all day and night. No news of our moving anywhere, and until strong detachments come up I expect we shall remain where we are.

The 90th are moving up, they say, and

on their arrival I suppose we shall be able to do something.

---

Cawnpore, *August* 24*th*, 1857.

I had so much to do yesterday that I had no time to write my usual letter; but I had no news to give you, so you did not lose anything.

Two men of the 16th Irregular Cavalry came in yesterday and laid down their arms. I do not know what Havelock intends doing with them, but I fancy they will be hanged. Poor Kenny of the 84th died this morning.

The steamer returned yesterday. All well. They were fired at several times, but no harm was done to anybody. A party of men are marching up from Allahabad, and we send away all our invalids to that place to-morrow by land. We are trying to get up some sports for the men, to distract their minds from hospitals, and doctors, etc. The band of the 84th have commenced playing, and ours practised this morning for the first time, so we are getting quite lively.

I had nearly 300 men for duty this morning, more than any other regiment in the Force. Tom Raikes is very much better, and I think is now quite out of danger; he had a narrow escape. Our men are rapidly getting better, and are daily improving on good rations and rest, luxuries they were getting strangers to altogether.

Breeks has sent up a very large present of Trichinopoly cigars for the use of the regiment; a most handsome present, and one which is highly appreciated by the men, who feel very deeply a kindness of the sort.

General Sir Patrick Grant has written a most complimentary letter to Neill about the " Lambs " on his departure from Calcutta, and we are *prouder* than ever.

I am writing this letter as hard as I can scribble, as you may see. Harcourt writes from Delhi, " We are getting on famously, if you don't look sharp we shall have destroyed the place before you come up."

I must now stop and go on with orderly room work.

---

Cawnpore, *August 27th*, 1857.

I have not written to you for the last two days, I literally have not had five minutes to myself. I have lots of news for you to-day, but you must not believe all you hear about anything, even when written by *me*, as every report is *improved* on in camp. *They say* that General Outram, instead of coming here, intends going to Lucknow, *via* Faizabad, with the 90th, 5th, and Ghoorkas; that 300 of the 50th have arrived in Allahabad, and the remainder, General Outram and 90th, were hourly expected, all *en route* for Cawnpore.

Two hundred of the 78th and fifty of *our* men are *really* coming up from Allahabad, and I believe Harris, Græme, Hornsby, Woods, "The Shepherd" and Duncan will come with them. We also expect Down and Parry very shortly, and we shall then have almost as many officers as men! *almost*. I also hear that Delhi was to be stormed *yesterday;* that I don't believe, as no general would give out to the public the time he intended storming a place.

The news from Lucknow is *very good*. They got lots of food in at the time the mutineers left them to attack us, and the only thing they want is tea and sugar for the poor women there, and these things cannot be procured. Everything else there seems to be really in very good plight.

The enemy are pushing lots of batteries all up the road from here to Lucknow, so we shall have to take a gun or two more before we get there.

The dress and silver salver I have still got by me. I do not like asking anyone to take them, as it is so very difficult to carry any personal property about. I wrote to Rean and asked him to do so, and afterwards felt ashamed of myself, so now I intend to send the dress by dawk as soon as I get some wax .cloth, which I hope to do in a day or two. Grant's wound is getting on well, and I hope he will be able to return to duty in a day or two. Seton goes to Allahabad with the rest of the sick and wounded to-night. Fraser only had a contused wound, and never suffered an hour from it—much the same with Gosling's scratch. Our men, I think, still pick up in health and well-being. But all the officers seem to be complaining more or less, and I really think that, by God's blessing, I am the most healthy officer of the Fusiliers in camp. I am perpetually trotting about from place to place, from morning till night. I fancy I have answered or acknowledged, half a hundred orders and chits from various folks since I began this letter. The whole of the army (officers) dine with the cavalry to-morrow night. We shall sit down upwards of a hundred at dinner. I must now stop, as I have to go to the adjutant-general's office to write orders.

Cawnpore, *August* 30*th*, 1857.

I was so idle and sleepy yesterday after the grand dinner at the cavalry mess, that I was yawning about all day over my work, and neglected to write my usual letter.

I must now tell you of this marvellous entertainment. Nearly ninety officers sat down to dinner in a large empty stable, and as every officer brought his own plates and tumblers, etc., and no two dishes or candlesticks on the table were of the same pattern, the effect was highly pleasing and original. They gave us, however, a capital dinner, and we made ourselves as jolly as possible—lots of speeches and songs, which all came off with more or less success. I absolutely sang! but not until Finlay of the 78th administered a bowl of whiskey punch, manufactured in a highly scientific and successful manner, and which we discussed with great gusto out of a jelly glass. I left at one o'clock, but some thirty or forty remained much later, and I rather think some must be there still. However, I was very sleepy when I got up and inspected the regiment at 4.30, and went to sleep after parade with infinite satisfaction, and so remained till 9 a.m.

We hear that Sir James Outram with 1500 men may be expected in about a fortnight. Two hundred men came in this morning from Allahabad, and we expect another party to-morrow.

We still have nothing but rain, and the ground is in an indescribable state of mud. In three weeks we shall have the cold weather, which we are all looking forward to in the fond expectation of getting strong and well again. We expect to start on or about the 10th of next month; this of course depends on the arrival of the detachments and regiments now *en route* for us. Raikes is much better, and gone to stop with Neill for a day or two.

---

Cawnpore, *September* 1st, 1857.

Gosling reported well this morning, so I had the most lively satisfaction of handing over the adjutancy to him. I am now a nobleman at large again. Barclay, " our gentle shepherd," arrived this morning with fifty-six of *our* men from Allahabad. With his party were eighty of the 78th, and fifty of the 84th, so we have nearly replaced the 300 sick and wounded that we sent away last week. Barclay is looking very well, and gorgeous in array. Ah! ah! that won't last long! The men's sports began last night, and they go on again to-day. Everything went off well yesterday, and our men hold their own very well among the other regiments in camp.

---

Cawnpore, *3rd September*, 1857.

A very hurried line to-day, as I have been on a committee all the morning about kits and bedding that have been lost in the field.

We hear to-day from England that 26,000 men leave for India, and two troops of horse artillery with six batteries. They will be a great thing. All quiet here, and I think the rains are really beginning to break up. Agra all well; we get despatches from there every day.

Several horse and pony races came off last evening with great éclat, and we are to have some more this evening. Our band and that of the 84th played last night, and the 78th play to-night for the first time.

We actually had a *lady* at the races last night. Poor woman! She escaped with her husband from Futtigharh, and they have been concealed by a rajah in Oude ever since; her escape is something miraculous—name Probyn, B.C.S. Other people arrived from the same place, but I have not heard what their names are, and have not seen them.

---

Cawnpore, *September 7th*, 1857.

We had most excellent news last night, both from Delhi and Lucknow. At the former place General Nicholson's brigade had engaged the Neemuch and Bareilly mutineers, and had beaten them with great slaughter, taking twelve guns from them.

At Lucknow garrison all well. The only two heavy guns belonging to the enemy dismounted, and they can neither fire nor move them. We also hear that the enemy have only one other serviceable gun (a 24-lb. iron gun), and that *we* hope to have the felicity of depriving them of next week. It is also said that only 4000 regular sepoys are left in arms in Oude; they get no pay, and have consequently dispersed and refuse to fight.

We expect to recross the river on Friday; but we shall not advance of course for a few days, as Sir James Outram cannot be here before the end of the week. The heat to-day is something awful—no a breath of air to be felt in house or tent.

---

Cawnpore, *September 8th*, 1857.

We had no dawk in from Madras this morning, and only got one newspaper from Calcutta with nothing in it, so I cannot give you much Bengal news. The troops now between this and Allahabad amount to 1490, and they say there are sixty *disbanded* officers with Sir James Outram. I suppose they will join the cavalry; and they will really be a most valuable acquisition. They are chiefly griffins and the officers of the Dinapore mutineers.

Our sports did not come off last night, but they are going to have a grand day next Thursday instead.

It is now said that we shall not cross the river on Friday, but that a portion of the force will cross on Sunday next: others say they know (on the highest authority of course) that we leave on the 20th.

The enemy have again begun to work at their batteries on the other side of the river, and I hear had a regular parade this morning with colours flying, and only three regiments and about 400 each.

Cawnpore, *September* 10*th*, 1857.

I did not write to you yesterday as I was on a committee all the day nearly, and felt so tired when I got back to my *stable* that I lay down and slept. I have not heard any fresh news. The Hon. J. Fraser, of the 1st B.N.I., and a Mr. Bennett of the same regiment, both joined our regiment this morning: Fraser seems a nice fellow. I do not yet know the other. Their regiment was one in garrison at Cawnpore. They were on detached duty at Bandah, from where they have apparently had a most miraculous escape. Their regiment fought against us at Cawnpore, and we have just heard that they are on the other side now, waiting for us with two other Cawnpore regiments.

The first is commanded by a soubadar who Fraser says always was a most troublesome character and for many years had shown a very discontented disposition.

I hope you still continue perfectly quiet at Madras, and have not been alarmed by any kind of disturbances. I feel so very very anxious, being at such a distance, and sometimes fancy all kinds of horrors.

I see by the papers that the 3rd Madras Cavalry have volunteered to go to Bengal!!! I hope they will not come! It is now worse than madness to trust any native. I feel more and more thankful that my luck got me to a European regiment. Officers here say nothing will induce them to serve with natives again under any circumstances: no wonder, after the awful treachery they have been all guilty of.

There was a grand paper hunt this morning, and I believe there was a very good meet, and they had a six mile run.

The rest of the games for the men come off to-morrow afternoon.

---

Cawnpore, *September* 13*th*, 1857.

We are making preparations for crossing the river, and we fired upon the enemy with our heavy guns this morning, and sent them running in all directions. 100 of our men go over to reconnoitre to-night, and I expect we shall be at Lucknow in less than a fortnight.

I only hope we shall not be left in Oude to garrison the different places there. If we are really intended to be relieved, we ought to be in Madras in January, but this I fear is far too good to be true. I expect that we shall not have so much fighting in Oude this time as we had when we were there last. The much larger force that we take with us will keep them at a respectful distance. A party of Outram's force have destroyed a party of 300 Oude men that crossed the river between this and Allahabad. He also destroyed two guns that they brought over with them. We expect his column in here the day after to-morrow, and by that time our bridge of boats ought to be in position, ready for us to cross, guns, commissariat, stores, etc., and then we shall be really off.

I must now wind up. To-morrow I shall be able to let you know the result of this evening's reconnaissance.

---

Cawnpore, *September* 14*th*, 1857.

Our men embarked in the steamer at a quarter to 3 p.m. yesterday, and steamed to within fifty yards of the opposite bank and there they struck on a sand-bank! All the world went down to see them start. And we all expected to see the enemy open fire on the steamer directly after the stoppage: but no, they kept at a very respectful distance. They all turned out of their camps and made a brave show, but they had no fight in them.

I waited there till nearly dark, and as Battine, an old schoolfellow of mine, was coming to dine with me at our mess (two miles off) I beat a retreat. Fraser and Arnold came into the mess tent very tired; they had done nothing, and had left Beaumont with twenty men to guard the steamer. Late last night an order came for the same men to go down to the steamer at 4.30 this morning. They went down again, and the steamer being still hard and fast, they crossed in boats and destroyed one of the enemy's batteries, and returned at twelve o'clock.

I have just been down there, and have seen Fraser, who says that they did not see a soul, but that just as they had got half way across the river on their return, one matchlock man rushed down to the water's edge, and fired wildly in the air. The bridge of boats is all ready, and I expect will be swung over the river tomorrow morning. Outram, with the 5th Fusiliers with Eyre's Battery and 100 Afghan horse, will be in to-morrow. We send our band out to play the Fusiliers in. The rest of the force will be here the day after. We have now (thanks to Olpherts) got one of our batteries horsed. I went out to see them manœuvre this morning, and I must say they worked most admirably. He has only had three weeks to get his horses in order, and his harness made, and they really looked very well indeed. We had intelligence yesterday from Candahar, Peshawur, Meerut, Delhi and Agra. From

Candahar we learn that the Persians have evacuated Herat, and from the other places "All well." News from Bombay bad: more than one corps have shown decided symptoms of revolt. We are all well now. The rain has ceased, and though the sun is very hot, we find *that* is better than the damp.

---

Cawnpore, *September* 15*th*, 1857.

The 5th Fusiliers, 400 men; 78th, 100; 84th, 15; 64th, 170, and a field battery of Artillery came in this morning, and we expect the 90th, some of the 5th, and a few horse will be in to-morrow. We are to be in two brigades. Ourselves, the 5th and 84th under General Neill, and the 78th and 90th and Sikhs under Colonel Hamilton. We expect to be in Lucknow in seven days. If the enemy do not fight better than they did before, we ought to walk through them very easily, and I make no doubt that we shall do so.

The orders have just been published and we parade to-morrow morning at 1.30 a.m. and take rations ready cooked with us for to-morrow. The Royal Artillery are attached to our Brigade. I am very glad of it. Maude and Maitland are both very nice fellows. We have had no Madras mail in, but I hope that I may get a letter from you to-morrow before I start; it will do me good. I shall not have many opportunities of writing from Oude this time. Outram says he wishes to get the affair over as quickly as possible, so we shall not be long away, and you will soon hear again regularly.

Cawnpore, *September* 17*th*, 1857.

At about 11 o'clock p.m. on the night of the 15th we were told that we had not to march at 2 a.m., and were to stand fast until further orders. This was the result of Outram's arrival, who said he would not have us exposed on the sandbanks on the other side of the river, and ordered the bridge of boats to be first attended to. This is now being done, and I fancy will be completed to-morrow morning.

We are now properly brigaded. Sikhs, 84th, 5th, and ourselves, Neill commanding : Captain Gordon, A.D.C., Captain Spurgin, Brigade Major, make 1st Brigade. 90th, 78th, and regiment of Ferozpore, Hamilton commanding, staff not yet appointed, 2nd Brigade and Artillery Brigade.

We all take our bands complete to make

as much noise as possible and show off at Lucknow. We (Fusiliers) are taking up lots of comforts for the ladies and children in our mess, even sugar plums for the children have not been rejected.

I have not yet seen General Outram, but intend calling this evening if I have time.

The English mail came in the day before yesterday. I got no letters, but am charmed at the interest that all ranks at home take in India and Indian affairs. Disraeli's speech very fine. The *Times* says that we may take any vengeance we like on the rebel sepoys. Very kind, but we intend doing so without the kind permission of the *Times*, and hope to be in at the death of a few of 'em before to-morrow night.

The Sikhs are by this time across the river. They left camp at eight this morning to cover the bridge of boats, island, etc.

I daresay they will have a scrimmage before the day is out.

Everybody is in high spirits and we hope to be back in less than a fortnight, and then we start for Agra and Delhi—which last place is a second Sebastopol and will give much trouble.

---

Cawnpore, *September* 18*th*, 1857.

At about 12 o'clock midnight, the Highland Brigade was ordered to the river and away they went, and I believe are now crossing. Maude has got some of his guns over to the island, and every now and again we hear him waking up his friends. We expect to get the order to be off every hour, and we are all packed and ready to move at a minute's notice.

We hear the most wonderful stories here

about the enemy. One is that two regiments sent over to Havelock yesterday to volunteer their services. Another that the garrison of Lucknow are now marching to Cawnpore under the protection of some powerful Rajahs and Zemindars. A third, that the mutineers turned their guns on each other—in fact repeated the celebrated Kilkenny Cat feat at Lucknow. Meanwhile we saw a reinforcement of 1500, and three guns, Horse Artillery, arrive in the enemy's camp yesterday. The guns we hope to have to-morrow. The men we shall in all probability dispose of otherwise.

I am writing this very early in the morning as we expect to be off at any moment.

We shall soon be back from Lucknow, and then I hope that something will be done to relieve us; at the same time I hardly expect it, as I know the 60th Rifles are not to come from Madras to Calcutta, and I see that our 2nd are still sending men from Burmah. However, you may be sure that everything will turn out for our good eventually, so we must look forward with brave hearts till happier days come.

THE END.

LONDON:
PRINTED BY GILBERT AND RIVINGTON, LD.,
ST. JOHN'S HOUSE, CLERKENWELL, E.C.

St. Dunstan's House, Fetter Lane,
London, E.C. 1894.

# Select List of Books in all Departments of Literature

PUBLISHED BY

**Sampson Low, Marston & Company, Ld.**

ABBEY, C. J., *Religious Thought in Old English Verse*, 8s. 6d.

—— and PARSONS, *Quiet Life*, from drawings; motive by Austin Dobson, 31s. 6d.

ABERDEEN, Earl of. See Prime Ministers.

ABNEY, Capt., and ·CUNNINGHAM, *Pioneers of the Alps*, new ed. 21s.

*About in the World*. See Gentle Life Series.

—— *Some Fellows*, by "an Eton boy," 2s. 6d.; new edit. 1s.

ADAMS, Charles K., *Historical Literature*, 12s. 6d.

*Ægean*. See "Fitzpatrick."

AINSLIE, P., *Priceless Orchid*, new ed., 3s. 6d. and 2s. 6d.

ALBERT, Prince. See Bay. S.

ALCOTT, L. M., *Jo's Boys*, 5s.

—— *Comic Tragedies*, 5s.

—— *Life, Letters and Journals*, by Ednah D. Cheney, 6s.; 3s. 6d. See also Low's Standard Series and Rose Library.

ALDAM, W. H., *Flies and Fly Making*, with actual flies on cardboard, 63s.

ALDEN, W. L. See Low's Standard Series.

ALFORD, Lady Marian, *Needlework as Art*, 21s.; l. p. 81s.

ALGER, J. G., *Englishmen in the French Revolution*, 6s.

—— *Glimpses of the French Revolution*, 6s.

*Amateur Angler in Dove Dale*, by E. M., 1s. 6d., 1s.

AMPHLETT, F. H., *Lower and Mid Thames, where and how to fish it*, 1s.

ANDERSEN, H.C., *Fairy Tales*, illust. by Scandinavian artists. 6s.

ANDERSON, W., *Pictorial Arts of Japan*, 4 parts, 168s.; artist's proofs, 252s.

*Angler's strange Experiences*, by Cotswold Isys, new edit., 3s. 6d.

ANNESLEY, C., *Standard Opera Glass*, 8th edit., 3s.

*Annual American Catalogue of Books*, 1886-93, each 15s., half morocco, 18s. each.

*Antipodean Notes*; a nine months' tour, by Wanderer, 7s. 6d.

APPLETON, *European Guide*, new edit., 2 parts, 10s. each.

*Arcadia*. Sidney's, new ed., 6s.

ARCHER, F., *How to write a Good Play*, buckram, 6s.

ARLOT'S *Coach Painting*, from the French by A. A. Fesquet, 6s.

ARMSTRONG, *South Pacific Fern Album*, actual fronds, 63s. net.

—— Isabel J., *Two Roving Englishwomen in Greece*, 6s.

ARMYTAGE, Hon. Mrs., *Wars of Queen Victoria's Reign*, 5s.
ARNOLD, *On the Indian Hills, Coffee Planting, &c.*, new ed., 7s. 6d.
—— R., *Ammonia and Ammonium Compounds*, illust. 5s.
*Artistic Japan*, text, woodcuts, and coloured plates, vols. I.-VI., 15s. each.
ASHE, R. P., *Two Kings of Uganda*, 6s.; new ed. 3s. 6d.
—— *Uganda, England's latest Charge*, stiff cover, 1s.
ATCHISON, C. C., *Winter Cruise in Summer Seas; "how I found" health*, illust., new ed. 7s. 6d.
ATKINSON, J. B., *Overbeck*. See Great Artists.
ATTWELL, *Italian Masters, especially in the National Gallery*, 3s. 6d.
AUDSLEY, G. A., *Chromolithography*, 44 coloured plates and text, 63s.
—— *Ornamental Arts of Japan*, 2 vols. morocco, 23l. 2s.; four parts, 15l. 15s.
—— W. and G. A., *Outlines of Ornament in all Styles*, 31s. 6d.
AUERBACH, B., *Brigitta* (B. Tauchnitz), 2s.; sewed, 1s. 6d.
—— *On the Height* (B. Tauchnitz), 3 vols. 6s.; sewed, 4s. 6d.
—— *Spinoza* (B. Tauchnitz), a novel, 2 vols. 4s.
AUSTRALIA. See F. Countries.
AUSTRIA. See F. Countries.
BACH. See Great Musicians.
BACON. See Eng. Philosophers.
—— Delia, *Biography*, 10s. 6d.
BADDELEY, W. St. Clair, *Love's Vintage; sonnets &c.*, 5s.
—— *Tchay and Chianti*, 5s.
—— *Travel-tide*, 7s. 6d.

BAKER, James, *John Westacott*, new edit. 3s. 6d.
—— *Foreign Competitors*, 1s. See also Low's Standard Novels.
—— R. Hindle, *Organist and Choirmaster's Diary*, 2s. 6d.
BALDWIN, James, *Story of Siegfried*, illust. 6s.
—— *Story of Roland*, illust. 6s.
—— *Story of the Golden Age*, illust. 6s.
*Ballad Stories*. See Bayard Series.
BALL, J. D., *Things Chinese*, new edit., 10s. 6d.
BALLANTYNE, T., *Essays*. See Bayard Series.
BAMFORD, A. J., *Turbans and Tails*, 7s. 6d.
BANCROFT, G., *History of America*, new edit. 6 vols. 73s. 6d.
—— *United S. Constitution, its Formation*, 2 vols., 24s.
*Barbizon Painters*. See Great Artists.
BARLOW, Alfred, *Weaving by Hand and Power*, new ed. 25s.
—— P. W., *Kaipara, New Z.*, 6s.
—— W., *Matter and Force*, 12s.
BARR, Amelia E., *Preacher's Daughter*, 5s.
BARROW, J., *Mountain Ascents (in England)*, new edit. 5s.
BARRY, J. W., *Corsican Studies*, 12s.; new edit. 6s.
BASSETT, *Legends of the Sea and Sailors*, 7s. 6d.
BATHGATE, A., *Waitaruna, a Story of New Zealand*, 5s.
*Bayard Series*, edited by the late J. Hain Friswell; flexible cloth extra, 2s. 6d. each.
Chevalier Bayard, by Berville.
St. Louis, by De Joinville.
Essays of Cowley.
Abdallah, by Laboullaye.

*Bayard Series—continued.*
Table-Talk of Napoleon.
Vathek, by Beckford.
Cavalier and Puritan Songs.
Words of Wellington.
Johnson's Rasselas.
Hazlitt's Round Table.
Browne's Religio Medici.
Ballad Stories of the Affections, by Robert Buchanan.
Coleridge's Christabel, &c.
Chesterfield's Letters.
Essays in Mosaic, by Ballantyne.
My Uncle Toby.
Rochefoucauld, Reflections.
Socrates, Memoirs from Xenophon.
Prince Albert's Golden Precepts.

BEACONSFIELD, *Public Life*, 3s. 6d.
—— See also Prime Ministers.

BEATTIE, T. R., *Pambaniso*, 6s.

BEAUGRAND, *Young Naturalists*, new edit. 5s.

BECKER, A.L., *First German Book*, 1s.; *Exercises*, 1s.; *Key* to both, 2s. 6d.; *Idioms*, 1s. 6d.

BECKFORD. See Bayard Series.

BEECHER, H. W., *Biography*, new edit. 10s. 6d.

BEETHOVEN. See Great Musicians.

BEHNKE, E., *Child's Voice*, 3s. 6d.

BELL, *Obeah, Witchcraft in the West Indies*, 2s. 6d., n. ed., 3s. 6d.

BERRY, C. A. See Preachers.

BERVILLE. See Bayard Series.

BIART, *Lucien*. See Low's Standard Books and Rose Library.

BICKERSTETH, ASHLEY, B.A., *Harmony of History*, 2s. 6d.
*Outlines of Roman History*, 2s. 6d.
—— E. and F., *Doing and Suffering*, new ed., 2s. 6d.
—— E. H., Bishop of Exeter, *Clergyman in his Home*, 1s.

BICKERSTETH, E. H., Bishop of Exeter, *From Year to Year*, original poetical pieces, morocco or calf, 10s. 6d.; padded roan, 5s.; roan, 5s.; cloth, 3s. 6d.
—— *Hymnal Companion to the Common Prayer*, full lists post free.
—— *Master's Home Call*, new edit. 1s.
—— *Octave of Hymns*, sewn, 3d., with music, 1s.
—— *The Reef, Parables*, illust. 7s. 6d. and 2s. 6d.
—— *Shadowed Home*, n. ed. 5s.
—— MISS M., *Japan as we saw it*, illust. from photos., 21s.

BIGELOW, JOHN, *France and the Confederate Navy*, 7s. 6d.

BILLROTH, *Care of the Sick*, 6s.

BIRD, F. J., *Dyer's Companion*, 42s.
——H.E., *Chess Practice*, n.e., 1s.

BLACK, WILLIAM. See Low's Standard Novels.

BLACKBURN, C. F., *Catalogue Titles, Index Entries, &c.* 14s.
—— *Rambles in Books*, cr. 8vo. 5s.; edit. de luxe, on handmade paper, only 50 copies, 15s.
—— H., *Art in the Mountains*, new edit. 5s.
—— *Artistic Travel*, 10s. 6d.
—— *Breton Folk*, n. e., 10s. 6d.

BLACKMORE, R. D, *Georgics of Virgil*, 4s. 6d.; cheap edit. 1s.
See also Low's Standard Novels.

BLAIKIE, *How to get Strong*, new edit. 5s.
—— *Sound Bodies for our Boys and Girls*, 2s. 6d.

BLOOMFIELD, ROBERT. See Choice Eds.

*Bobby, a Story*, by Vesper, 1s.
BOCK, *Temples & Elephants*, 21s.
BONWICK, JAMES, *Colonial Days*, 2s. 6d.

BONWICK, JAMES, *Colonies,* 1s. ea.; 1 vol. 5s.
—— *Daily Life of the Tasmanians,* 12s. 6d.
—— *First Twenty Years of Australia,* 5s.
—— *Last of the Tasmanians,* 16s.
—— *Port Philip,* 21s.
—— *Lost Tasmanian Race,* 4s.
BOSANQUET, C., *Blossoms from the King's Garden,* 6s.
—— *Jehoshaphat,* 1s.
—— *Lenten Meditations,* Ser. I. 1s. 6d.; II. 2s.
—— *Tender Grass for Lambs,* 2s. 6d.
BOULTON, N. W. *Rebellions,* Canadian life, 9s.
BOURKE, *On the Border with Crook,* illust., roy. 8vo, 21s.
—— *Snake Dance of Arizona,* with coloured plates, 21s.
BOUSSENARD. See Low's Standard Books.
BOWEN, F., *Modern Philosophy,* new ed. 16s.
BOWER, G. S., and WEBB, *Law of Electric Lighting,* 12s. 6d.
BOWNE, R. P., *Metaphysics,* 12s. 6d.
BOYESEN, H. H., *Against Heavy Odds,* 5s.; also 3s. 6d.
—— *History of Norway,* 7s. 6d.
—— *Modern Vikings,* 6s.; also 3s. 6d.
*Boy's Froissart, King Arthur, Percy,* see "Lanier."
*Boys,* first yearly vol. 7s. 6d.
BRADSHAW, *New Zealand as it is,* 12s. 6d.
—— *New Zealand of To-day,* 14s.
BRANNT, *Fats and Oils,* 42s.
—— *Scourer and Dyer,* 10s. 6d.
—— *Soap and Candles,* 35s.
—— *Vinegar, Acetates,* 25s.

BRANNT, *Distillation of Alcohol,* 12s. 6d.
—— *Metal Worker's Receipts,* 12s. 6d.
—— *Metallic Alloys,* 12s. 6d.
—— and ANDRES, *Varnishes,* 12s. 6d.
—— and WAHL, *Techno-Chemical Receipt Book,* 10s. 6d.
BRETON, JULES, *Life of an Artist,* an autobiography, 7s. 6d.
BRETT, EDWIN J., *Ancient Arms and Armour,* 105s. nett.
BRISSE, *Menus and Recipes,* French and English, new edit. 5s.
*Britons in Brittany,* 2s. 6d.
BROOKS, NOAH, *Boy Settlers,* 6s.; new ed., 3s. 6d.
BROWN, A. J., *Rejected of Men,* and other poems, 3s. 6d.
—— A. S. *Madeira and Canary Islands for Invalids,* n. ed. 2s. 6d.
—— RICHARD, *Northern Atlantic,* for travellers, 4s. 6d.
—— ROBERT. See Low's Standard Novels.
*Brown's South Africa,* 2s. 6d.
BROWNE, LENNOX, and BEHNKE, *Voice, Song, & Speech,* 15s.; new edit. 5s.
—— *Voice Use,* 3s. 6d.
—— SIR T. See Bayard Series.
BRYCE, G., *Manitoba,* 7s. 6d.
—— *Short History of the Canadian People,* 7s. 6d.
BUCHANAN, R. See Bayard.
BULKELEY, OWEN T., *Lesser Antilles,* 2s. 6d.
BUNYAN. See Low's Standard Series.
BURDETT-COUTTS, *Brookfield Stud,* 5s.
—— BARONESS, *Woman's Mission,* Congress papers, 10s. 6d.

BURNABY, Evelyn, *Ride from Land's End to John o' Groats*, 3s. 6d.
—— Mrs., *High Alps in Winter*, 14s.
BURNLEY, James, *History of Wool and Wool-combing*, 21s.
BUTLER, Col. Sir W. F., *Campaign of the Cataracts*, 18s.
—— See also Low's Standard Books.
BUXTON, Ethel M. Wilmot, *Wee Folk*, 5s.
BYNNER. See Low's Standard Novels.
CABLE, G. W., *Bonaventure*, 5s.
CADOGAN, Lady Adelaide, *Drawing-room Comedies*, illust. 10s. 6d., acting edit. 6d.
—— *Illustrated Games of Patience*, col. diagrams, 12s. 6d.
—— *New Games of Patience*, with coloured diagrams, 12s. 6d.
CAHUN. See Low's Standard Books.
CALDECOTT, Randolph, *Memoir*, by Henry Blackburn, new edit. 7s. 6d. and 5s.
—— *Sketches*, pict. bds. 2s. 6d.
CALL, Annie Payson, *Power through Repose*, 3s. 6d.
CALLAN, H., M.A., *Wanderings on Wheel and Foot through Europe*, 1s. 6d.
CALVERT, Edward (artist), *Memoir and Writings*, imp. 4to, 63s. nett.
*Cambridge Trifles*, 2s. 6d.
*Cambridge Staircase*, 2s. 6d.
CAMPBELL, Lady Colin, *Book of the Running Brook*, 5s.
—— T. See Choice Editions.
CANTERBURY, Archbishop. See Preachers.
*Capitals of the World*, plates and text, 2 vols., 4to, half morocco, gilt edges, 63s. nett.

CARBUTT, Mrs., *Five Months Fine Weather; Canada, U.S. and Mexico*, 5s.
CARLETON, Will, *City Ballads*, illust. 12s. 6d.
—— *City Legends*, ill. 12s. 6d.
—— *Farm Festivals*, ill. 12s. 6d.
—— *City Ballads*, 1s. ⎫
—— *City Legends*, 1s. ⎬ 1 vol., 3s. 6d.
—— *City Festivals*, 1s. ⎭
—— *Farm Ballads*, 1s. ⎫
—— *Farm Festivals*, 1s. ⎬ 1 vol., 3s. 6.
—— *Farm Legends*, 1s. ⎭
—— *Poems*, 6 vols. in case, 8s.
—— See also Rose Library.
CARNEGIE, Andrew, *American Four-in-hand in Britain*, 10s. 6d.; also 1s.
—— *Triumphant Democracy*, 6s.; new edit. 1s. 6d.; paper, 1s.
CAROVÉ, *Story without an End*, illust. by E. V. B., 7s. 6d.
CARPENTER. See Preachers.
CAVE, *Picturesque Ceylon*, 21s. nett.
*Celebrated Racehorses*, fac-sim. portraits, 4 vols., 126s.
CÉLIÈRE. See Low's Standard Books.
*Changed Cross, &c.*, poems, 2s. 6d.
*Chant-book Companion to the Common Prayer*, 2s.; organ ed. 4s.
CHAPIN, *Mountaineering in Colorado*, 10s. 6d.
CHAPLIN, J. G., *Bookkeeping*, 2s. 6d.
CHARLES, J. T. See Playtime Library.
CHATTOCK, *Notes on Etching*, new edit. 10s. 6d.
CHENEY, A. N., *Fishing with the Fly*, 12s. 6d.

CHERUBINI. See Great Musicians.

CHESTERFIELD. See Bayard Series.

*Choice Editions of choice books,* illustrated by Cope, Creswick, Birket Foster, Horsley, Harrison Weir, &c., cloth extra gilt, gilt edges, 2s. 6d. each; re-issue, 1s. each.

Bloomfield's Farmer's Boy.
Campbell's Pleasures of Hope.
Coleridge's Ancient Mariner.
Elizabethan Songs and Sonnets.
Goldsmith's Deserted Village.
Goldsmith's Vicar of Wakefield.
Gray's Elegy in a Churchyard.
Keats' Eve of St. Agnes.
Milton's Allegro.
Poetry of Nature, by H. Weir.
Rogers' Pleasures of Memory.
Shakespeare's Songs and Sonnets.
Tennyson's May Queen.
Wordsworth's Pastoral Poems.

CHURCH, W. C., *Life of Ericsson,* new ed., 16s.

CHURCHILL, LORD RANDOLPH, *Men, Mines and Animals in South Africa,* 21s.; new ed. 6s.

CLARK, Mrs. K. M., *Southern Cross Fairy Tale,* 5s.

—— *Persephone and other Poems,* 5s.

CLARKE, C. C., *Recollections of Writers, with Letters,* 10s. 6d.

—— PERCY, *Three Diggers,* 6s.

—— *Valley Council;* from T. Bateman's Journal, 6s.

*Claude le Lorrain.* See Great Artists.

COCHRAN, W., *Pen and Pencil in Asia Minor,* 21s.

COLERIDGE, S.T. See Choice Editions and Bayard Series.

COLLINGWOOD, H. See Low's Standard Books.

COLLYER, ROBERT, *Things Old and New,* Sermons, 5s.

CONDER, J., *Flowers of Japan and Decoration,* coloured Plates, 42s. nett.

—— *Landscape Gardening in Japan,* 52s.6d. nett.; supplement. 36s. nett.

CORDINGLEY, W. G., *Guide to the Stock Exchange,* 2s.

CORREGGIO. See Great Artists.

COWEN, JOSEPH, M.P., *Life and Speeches,* 14s.

COWLEY. See Bayard Series.

COX, DAVID. See Great Artists.

—— J. CHARLES, *Gardens of Scripture; Meditations,* 5s.

COZZENS, F., *American Yachts,* pfs. 21l.; art. pfs. 31l. 10s.

—— S. W. See Low's Standard Books.

CRADDOCK. See Low's Standard Novels.

CRAIK, D., *Millwright and Miller,* 21s.

CROCKER, *Education of the Horse,* 8s. 6d. nett.

CROKER, MRS. B. M. See Low's Standard Novels.

CROSLAND, MRS. NEWTON, *Landmarks of a Literary Life,* 7s. 6d.

CROUCH, A. P., *Glimpses of Feverland* (West Africa), 6s.

—— *On a Surf-bound Coast,* 7s. 6d.; new edit. 5s.

CRUIKSHANK, G. See Great Artists.

CUDWORTH, W., *Abraham Sharp, Mathematician,* 26s.

CUMBERLAND, STUART. See Low's Standard Novels.

CUNDALL, J., *Shakespeare,* 3s. 6d., 5s. and 2s.

CURTIS, C. B., *Velazquez and Murillo,* with etchings, 31s. 6d.; large paper, 63s.

CURTIS, W. E., *Capitals of Spanish America*, 18s.

CUSHING, W., *Anonyms*, 2 vols. 52s. 6d.

—— W., *Initials and Pseudonyms*, 25s.; ser. II., 21s.

CUTCLIFFE, H. C., *Trout Fishing*, new edit. 3s. 6d.

DALY, MRS. DOMINIC, *Digging, Squatting in N. S. Australia*, 12s.

DANTE, *Text-book in Four Languages*, illum. cover, 5s. nett.

D'ANVERS, N., *Architecture and Sculpture*, new edit. 5s.

—— *Elementary Art, Architecture, Sculpture, Painting*, new edit. 12s. and 10s. 6d.

—— *Painting*, new ed. by F. Cundall, 6s.

DAUDET, ALPHONSE, *Port Tarascon*, by H. James, 7s. 6d.; also 5s. and 3s. 6d.

DAVIES, C., *Modern Whist*, 4s.

DAVIS, C. T., *Manufacture of Leather*, 52s. 6d.

—— *Manufacture of Paper*, 28s.

—— *Manufacture of Bricks*, 25s.

—— *Steam Boiler Incrustation*, 8s. 6d.

—— G. B., *International Law*, 10s. 6d.

DAWIDOWSKY, *Glue, Gelatine, Veneers, Cements*, 12s. 6d.

*Day of my Life*, by an Eton boy, new edit. 2s. 6d.; also 1s.

*Days in Clover*, by the "Amateur Angler," 1s.; illust., 2s. 6d.

DELLA ROBBIA. See Great Artists.

*Denmark and Iceland.* See Foreign Countries.

DENNETT, R. E., *Seven Years among the Fjort*, 7s. 6d.

DERRY (B. of). See Preachers.

DE WINT. See Great Artists.

DIGGLE, J. W., *Bishop Fraser's Lancashire Life*, new edit. 12s. 6d.; popular ed. 3s. 6d.

—— *Sermons for Daily Life*, 5s.

DIRUF, O., *Kissingen*, 5s. and 3s. 6d.

DOBSON, AUSTIN, *Hogarth*, with a bibliography, &c., of prints, illust. 24s.; l. paper 52s. 6d.; new ed. 12s. 6d.

—— See also Great Artists.

DOD, *Peerage, Baronetage, and Knightage, for 1894*, 10s. 6d.

DODGE, MRS., *Hans Brinker*. See Low's Standard Books.

*Doing and Suffering; memorials of E. and F. Bickersteth*, new ed., 2s. 6d.

DONKIN, J. G., *Trooper and Redskin*; Canada police, 8s. 6d.

DONNELLY, IGNATIUS, *Atlantis, the Antediluvian World*, new edit. 12s. 6d.

—— *Cæsar's Column*, authorised edition, 3s. 6d.

—— *Doctor Huguet*, 3s. 6d.

—— *Great Cryptogram*, Bacon's Cipher in the so-called Shakspere Plays, 2 vols., 30s.

—— *Ragnarok: the Age of Fire and Gravel*, 12s. 6d.

DORE, GUSTAVE, *Life and Reminiscences*, by Blanche Roosevelt, fully illust. 24s.

DOS PASSOS, J. R., *Law of Stockbrokers and Exchanges*, 35s.

DOUGALL, J. D., *Shooting Appliances, Practice*, n. ed. 7s. 6d.

DOUGLAS, JAMES, *Bombay and Western India*, 2 vols., 42s. nett.

DU CHAILLU, PAUL. See Low's Standard Books.

DUFFY, SIR C. G., *Conversations with Carlyle*, 6s.

DUNCKLEY ("Verax.") See Prime Ministers.
DUNDERDALE, GEORGE, *Prairie and Bush*, 6s.
Dürer. See Great Artists.
DYKES, J. Osw. See Preachers.
EBERS, G., *Per Aspera*, 2 vols., 21s.; new ed., 2 vols., 4s.
*Echoes from the Heart*, 3s. 6d.
EDEN, C. H. See For. Countries.
EDMONDS, C., *Poetry of the Anti-Jacobin*, new edit. 7s. 6d.; large paper, 21s.
EDWARDS, *American Steam Engineer*, 12s. 6d.
—— *Modern Locomotive Engines*, 12s. 6d.
—— *Steam Engineer's Guide*, 12s. 6d.
—— H. S. See Great Musicians.
—— M. B., *Dream of Millions, &c.*, 1s.
—— See also Low's Standard Novels.
EDWORDS. *Camp Fires of a Naturalist, N. Am. Mammals*, 6s.
EGGLESTON, G. CARY, *Juggernaut*, 6s.
*Egypt.* See Foreign Countries.
*Elizabethan Songs.* See Choice Editions.
EMERSON, Dr. P. H., *English Idylls*, new ed., 2s.
—— *Naturalistic Photography*, new edit. 5s.
—— *Pictures of East Anglian Life*; plates and vignettes, 105s.; large paper, 147s.
—— *Son of the Fens*, 6s.
—— See also Low's 1s. Novels.
—— and GOODALL, *Life on the Norfolk Broads*, plates, 126s.; large paper, 210s.
—— and GOODALL, *Wild Life on a Tidal Water*, copper plates, ord. edit. 25s.; édit. de luxe, 63s.
EMERSON, RALPH WALDO, *In Concord*, a memoir by E. W. Emerson, 7s. 6d.
*English Catalogue*, 1863-71, 42s.; 1872-80, 42s.; 1881-9, 52s. 6d.; 1890-93, 5s.
*English Catalogue, Index vol.* 1837-56, 26s.; 1856-76, 42s.; 1874-80, 18s.; 1881-89, 31s. 6d.
*English Philosophers*, edited by E. B. Ivan Müller, 3s. 6d. each.
Bacon, by Fowler.
Hamilton, by Monck.
Hartley and James Mill, by Bower.
Shaftesbury & Hutcheson; Fowler.
Adam Smith, by J. A. Farrer.
*English Readers.* See Low.
ERCKMANN-CHATRIAN. See Low's Standard Books.
ESLER, E. RENTOUL, *The Way they Loved at Grimpat*, 3s. 6d.
ESMARCH, F., *Handbook of Surgery*, with 647 new illust. 21s.
*Essays on English Writers.* See Gentle Life Series.
EVANS, G. E., *Repentance of Magdalene Despar, &c.*, poems, 5s.
—— S. & F., *Upper Ten*, a story, 1s.
—— W. E., *Songs of the Birds, Analogies of Spiritual Life*, 6s.
EVELYN. See Low's Stand. Books.
—— JOHN, *Life of Mrs. Godolphin*, 7s. 6d.
EVES, C. W., *West Indies*, n. ed. 7s. 6d.
FAGAN, L., *History of Engraving in England*, illust. from rare prints, £25 nett.
FAIRBAIRN. See Preachers.
*Faith and Criticism*; Essays by Congregationalists, 6s.

*Familiar Words.* See Gentle Life Series.

FARINI, G. A., *Through the Kalahari Desert*, 21s.

FAWCETT, *Heir to Millions*, 6s.

—— See also Rose Library.

FAY, T., *Three Germanys*, 2 vols. 35s.

FEILDEN, H. ST. J., *Some Public Schools*, 2s. 6d.

—— Mrs., *My African Home*, 7s. 6d.

FENN, G. MANVILLE. *Black Bar*, illust. 5s.

—— *Fire Island*, 6s.

—— See also Low's Stand. Bks.

FFORDE, B., *Subaltern, Policeman, and the Little Girl*, 1s.

—— *Trotter, a Poona Mystery*, 1s.

FIELDS, JAMES T., *Memoirs*, 12s. 6d.

—— *Yesterdays with Authors*, 16s.; also 10s. 6d.

*Figure Painters of Holland.* See Great Artists.

FINCK, HENRY T., *Pacific Coast Scenic Tour*, fine pl. 10s. 6d.

FISHER, G. P., *Colonial Era in America*, 7s. 6d.

FITZGERALD. See Foreign Countries.

—— PERCY, *Book Fancier*, 5s.; large paper, 12s. 6d.

FITZPATRICK, T., *Autumn Cruise in the Ægean*, 10s. 6d.

—— *Transatlantic Holiday*, 10s. 6d.

FLEMING, S., *England and Canada*, 6s.

*Fly Fisher's Register of Date, Place, Time Occupied, Flies Observed, wind, weather, &c.*, 4s.

FOLKARD, R., *Plant Lore, Lejends and Lyrics*, n. ed., 10s. 6d.

*Foreign Countries and British Colonies*, descriptive handbooks edited by F. S. Pulling, 3s. 6d.
Australia, by Fitzgerald.
Austria-Hungary, by Kay.
Denmark and Iceland, by E. C. Otté.
Egypt, by S. L. Poole.
France, by Miss Roberts.
Germany, by S. Baring Gould.
Greece, by L. Sergeant.
Japan, by Mossman.
Peru, by Clements R. Markham.
Russia, by Morfill.
Spain, by Webster.
Sweden and Norway, by Woods.
West Indies, by C. H. Eden.

FOREMAN, J., *Philippine Islands*, 21s.

FRA ANGELICO. See Great Artists.

FRA BARTOLOMMEO, ALBERTINELLI, and ANDREA DEL SARTO. See Great Artists.

FRANC, MAUD JEANNE, *Beatrice Melton*, 4s.

—— *Emily's Choice*, n. ed. 5s.

—— *Golden Gifts*, 4s.

—— *Hall's Vineyard*, 4s.

—— *Into the Light*, 4s.

—— *John's Wife*, 4s.

—— *Little Mercy; for better, for worse*, 4s.

—— *Marian, a Tale*, n. ed. 5s.

—— *Master of Ralston*, 4s.

—— *Minnie's Mission, a Temperance Tale*, 4s.

—— *No longer a Child*, 4s.

—— *Silken Cords, a Tale*, 4s.

—— *Two Sides to Every Question*, 4s.

—— *Vermont Vale*, 5s.

*A plainer edition is issued at* 2s. 6d.

*France.* See Foreign Countries.

*Frank's Ranche; or, My Holiday in the Rockies*, n. ed. 5s.

FRASER, Sir W. A., *Hic et ubique*, 3s. 6d.; large paper, 21s.

FREEMAN, J., *Melbourne Life, lights and shadows,* 6s.
*French and English Birthday Book*, by Kate D. Clark, 7s. 6d.
*French Readers.* See Low.
*Fresh Woods and Pastures New*, by the Amateur Angler, 5s., 1s. 6d., 1s.
FRIEZE, *Duprè, Florentine Sculptor*, 7s. 6d.
FRISWELL. See Gentle Life.
*Froissart for Boys.* See Lanier.
FROUDE, J. A. See Prime Ministers.
*Gainsborough and Constable.* See Great Artists.
GARLAND, HAMLIN, *Prairie Folks*, 6s.
GASPARIN, *Sunny Fields and Shady Woods*, 6s.
GEFFCKEN, *British Empire,* translated, 7s. 6d.
*Gentle Life Series*, edited by J. Hain Friswell, sm. 8vo, 6s. per vol.; calf extra, 10s. 6d. ea.; 16mo, 2s. 6d., except when price is given.
Gentle Life.
About in the World.
Like unto Christ.
Familiar Words, 6s.; also 3s. 6d.
Montaigne's Essays.
Gentle Life, second series.
Silent hour; essays.
Half-length Portraits.
Essays on English Writers.
Other People's Windows, 6s. & 2s. 6d.
A Man's Thoughts.
*Germany.* See For. Countries.
GESSI, ROMOLO PASHA, *Seven Years in the Soudan*, 18s.
GHIBERTI & DONATELLO. See Great Artists.
GIBBS, W. A., *Idylls of the Queen*, 1s., 5s., & 3s.; Prelude, 1s.
GIBSON, W. H., *Happy Hunting Grounds*, 31s. 6d.

GILES, E., *Australia Twice Traversed*, 1872-76, 2 vols. 30s.
GILL, J. See Low's Readers.
GILLIAT. See Low's Stand. Novels.
*Giotto*, by Harry Quilter, illust. 15s.
—— See also Great Artists.
GLADSTONE. See Prime Ministers.
GLAVE, E. J., *Congoland, Six Years' Adventure*, 7s. 6d.
*Goethe's Faustus,* in the original rhyme, by Alfred H. Huth, 5s.
—— *Prosa*, by C. A. Buchheim (Low's German Series), 3s. 6d.
GOLDSMITH, O., *She Stoops to Conquer*, by Austin Dobson, illust. by E. A. Abbey, 84s.
—— See also Choice Editions.
GOOCH, FANNY C., *Face to Face with the Mexicans*, 16s.
GOODMAN, E. J., *The Best Tour in Norway,* new edit., 7s. 6d.
GOODYEAR, W. H., *Grammar of the Lotus, Ornament and Sun Worship*, 63s. nett.
GORDON, E. A., *Clear Round, Story from other Countries*, 7s. 6d.
—— J. E. H., *Physical Treatise on Electricity and Magnetism*, 3rd ed. 2 vols. 42s.
—— *Electric Lighting,* 18s.
—— *School Electricity*, 5s.
—— Mrs. J. E. H., *Decorative Electricity,* illust. 12s.; n. ed. 6s.
—— *Eunice Anscombe*, 7s. 6d.
GOT (E.) *Comedie Française à Londres*, 3s.
GOULD, S. B. See Foreign Countries.
*Gounod, Life and Works,* 10s. 6d.
GOWER, LORD RONALD. See Great Artists.

GRAESSI, *Italian Dictionary,* 3s. 6d.; roan, 5s.

GRAY, T. See Choice Eds.

*Great Artists,* Illustrated Biographies, 3s. 6d. per vol. except where the price is given.
Barbizon School, 2 vols.; 1 vol. 7s. 6d.
Claude le Lorrain.
Correggio, 2s. 6d.
Cox and De Wint.
George Cruikshank.
Della Robbia and Cellini, 2s. 6d.
Albrecht Dürer.
Figure Painters of Holland. By Lord Ronald Gower.
Fra Angelico, Masaccio, &c.
Fra Bartolommeo; Leader Scott.
Gainsborough and Constable.
Ghiberti and Donatello, by Leader Scott, 2s. 6d.
Giotto, by H. Quilter; 4to, 15s.
Hogarth, by Austin Dobson.
Hans Holbein.
Landscape Painters of Holland.
Landseer, by F. G. Stephens.
Leonardo da Vinci, by J. P. Richter.
Little Masters of Germany, by W. B. Scott; éd. de luxe, 10s. 6d.
Mantegna and Francia.
Meissonier, 2s. 6d.
Michelangelo.
Mulready.
Murillo, by Ellen E. Minor, 2s. 6d.
Overbeck, by J. B. Atkinson.
Raphael, by N. D'Anvers.
Rembrandt, by J. W. Mollett.
Reynolds, by F. S. Pulling.
Romney and Lawrence, 2s. 6d.
Rubens, by Kett.
Tintoretto, by Osler.
Titian, by Heath.
Turner, by Monkhouse.
Vandyck and Hals, by P. R. Head.
Velasquez, by Edwin Stowe.
Vernet & Delaroche.
Watteau, by Mollett, 2s. 6d.
Wilkie, by Mollett.

*Great Musicians,* biographies, edited by F. Hueffer, 3s. each:—
Bach, by Poole.
Beethoven.

*Great Musicians*—continued.
Cherubini.
English Church Composers
Handel.
Haydn.
Mendelssohn.
Mozart.
Purcell.
Rossini, &c., by H. Sutherland Edwards.
Schubert.
Schumann.
Richard Wagner.
Weber.

*Greece.* See Foreign Countries.

GRIEB, *German Dictionary,* n. ed. 2 vols., fine paper, cloth, 21s.

GROHMANN, *Camps in the Rockies,* 12s. 6d.

GROVES. See Low's Std. Bks.

GROWOLL, A., *Profession of Bookselling,* pt. I., 9s. nett.

GULLIE. *Instruction and Amusements of the Blind,* ill., 5s.

GUIZOT, *History of England,* illust. 3 vols. re-issue, 10s. 6d. ea.

—— *History of France,* illust. re-issue, 8 vols. 10s. 6d. each.

—— Abridged by G. Masson, 5s.

GUYON, Madame, *Life,* 6s.

HADLEY, J., *Roman Law,* 7s. 6d.

HALE, *How to Tie Salmon-Flies,* 12s. 6d.

*Half-length Portraits.* See Gentle Life Series.

HALFORD, F. M., *Dry Fly-fishing,* n. ed. 25s.

—— *Floating Flies,* 15s. & 30s.

HALL, *How to Live Long,* 2s.

HALSEY, F. A., *Slide Valve Gears,* 8s. 6d.

HAMILTON. See English Philosophers.

—— E. *Fly-fishing for Salmon,* 6s.; large paper, 10s. 6d.

—— *Riverside Naturalist,* 14s.

HANDEL. See G. Musicians.
HANDS, T., *Numerical Exercises in Chemistry*, 2s. 6d.; without ans. 2s.; ans. sep. 6d.
*Handy Guide to Dry-fly Fishing*, by Cotswold Isys, new ed., 1s.
*Handy Guide Book to Japanese Islands*, 6s. 6d.
HARKUT. See Low's Stand. Novels.
HARLAND, MARION, *Home Kitchen, Receipts*, &c., 5s.
HARRIS, W. B., *Land of an African Sultan*, 10s. 6d.; large paper, 31s. 6d.
HARRISON, MARY, *Modern Cookery*, 6s.
—— *Skilful Cook*, n. ed. 5s.
—— W., *London Houses*, Illust. 6s. net; n. edit., 2s. 6d.
—— *Memor. Paris Houses*, 6s.
HARTLEY and MILL. See English Philosophers.
HATTON. See Low's Standard Novels.
HAWEIS, H. R., *Broad Church*, 6s.
—— *Poets in the Pulpit*, new edit. 6s.; also 3s. 6d.
—— Mrs., *Housekeeping*, 2s. 6d.
—— *Beautiful Houses*, n. ed. 1s.
HAYDN. See Great Musicians.
HAZLITT. See Bayard Ser.
HEAD, PERCY R. See Illus. Text Books and Great Artists.
HEARN, L., *Youma*, 5s.
HEATH, F. G., *Fern World*, col. plates, 12s. 6d., new edit. 6s.
—— GERTRUDE, *Tell us Why*, 2s. 6d.
HEGINBOTHAM, *Stockport*, I., II., III., IV., V., 10s. 6d. each.
HELDMANN, B. See Low's Standard Books for Boys.

HENTY, G. A. See Low's Standard Books for Boys.
—— RICHMOND, *Australiana*, 5s.
HERRICK, R., *Poetry Edited by Austin Dobson*, illust. by E. A. Abbey, 42s.
HERVEY, GEN., *Records of Crime, Thuggee, &c.*, 2 vols., 30s.
HICKS, C. S., *Our Boys, and what to do with Them; Merchant Service*, 5s.
—— *Yachts, Boats, and Canoes, Design and Construction*, 10s. 6d.
HILL, G. B., *Footsteps of Johnson*, 63s.; édition de luxe, 117s.
—— KATHARINE ST., *Grammar of Palmistry*, new ed., 1s.
HINMAN, R., *Eclectic Physical Geography*, 5s.
*Hints on proving Wills without Professional Assistance*, n. ed. 1s.
*Historic Bindings in the Bodleian Library*, many plates, 94s. 6d., 84s., 52s. 6d. and 42s.
HODDER, E., *History of South Australia*, 2 vols., 24s.
HOEY, Mrs. CASHEL. See Low's Standard Novels.
HOFFER, *Caoutchouc & Gutta Percha*, by W. T. Brannt, 12s. 6d.
HOGARTH. See Gr. Artists, and Dobson, Austin.
HOLBEIN. See Great Artists.
HOLDER, CHARLES F., *Ivory King*, 8s. 6d.; new ed. 3s. 6d.
—— *Living Lights*, n. ed. 3s. 6d.
HOLM, SAXE, *Draxy Miller*, See Low's Standard Series.
HOLMAN, T., *Life in the Navy*, 1s.
—— *Salt Yarns*, new ed., 1s.
HOLMES, O. WENDELL, *Before the Curfew*, 5s.
—— *Over the Tea Cups*, 6s.

HOLMES, O. WENDELL, *Iron Gate, &c., Poems*, 6s.
—— *Last Leaf*, holiday vol., 42s.
—— *Mechanism in Thought and Morals*, 1s. 6d.
—— *Mortal Antipathy*, 8s. 6d., 2s. and 1s.
—— *Our Hundred Days in Europe*, new edit. 6s. and 3s. 6d.; large paper, 15s.
—— *Poetical Works*, new edit., 2 vols. 10s. 6d.
—— *Works*, prose, 10 vols.; poetry, 3 vols.; 13 vols. 84s. Limited large paper edit., 14 vols. 294s. nett.
—— See also Low's Standard Novels and Rose Library.
*Homer, Iliad*, translated by A. Way, vol. I., 9s.; II., 9s.; *Odyssey*, in English verse, 7s. 6d.
*Horace in Latin*, with Smart's literal translation, 2s. 6d.; translation only, 1s. 6d.
HOSMER, J., *German Literature, a short history*, 7s. 6d.
*How and where to Fish in Ireland*, by Hi-Regan, 3s. 6d.
HOWARD, BLANCHE W., *Tony the Maid*, 3s. 6d.
—— See also Low's Standard Novels.
HOWELLS, W. D. *Undiscovered Country*, 3s. 6d. and 1s.
HOWORTH, SIR H. H., *Glacial Nightmare & the Flood*, 2 vols., 30s.
—— *Mammoth and the Flood*, 18s.
HUBERT. See Men of Achievem.
HUEFFER. E. See Great Musicians.
HUGHES, HUGH PRICE. See Preachers.
HUME, FERGUS, *Creature of the Night*, 1s. See also Low's Standard Novels and 1s. Novels.

HUMFREY, MARIAN, *Obstetric Nursing*, 3s. 6d.
*Humorous Art at the Naval Exhibition*, 1s.
HUMPHREYS, JENNET, *Some Little Britons in Brittany*, 2s. 6d.
HUNTINGDON, *The Squire's Nieces*, 2s. 6d. (Playtime Library.)
HYDE, *A Hundred Years by Post, Jubilee Retrospect*, 1s.
*Hymnal Companion to the Book of Common Prayer*, separate lists gratis.
*Iceland*. See Foreign Countries.
*Illustrated Text-Books of Art-Education*, edit. by E. J. Poynter, R.A., 5s. each.
Architecture, Classic and Early Christian, by Smith and Slater.
Architecture, Gothic and Renaissance, by T. Roger Smith.
German, Flemish, and Dutch Painting.
Painting, Classic and Italian, by Head, &c.
Painting, English and American.
Sculpture, modern; Leader Scott.
Sculpture, by G. Redford.
Spanish and French artists; Smith.
Water Colour Painting, by Redgrave.
INDERWICK, F. A., *Interregnum*, 10s. 6d.
—— *Prisoner of War*, 5s.
—— *King Edward and New Winchelsea*.
—— *Sidelights on the Stuarts*, new edit. 7s. 6d.
INGELOW, JEAN. See Low's Standard Novels.
INGLIS, HON. JAMES, *Our New Zealand Cousins*, 6s.
—— *Sport and Work on the Nepaul Frontier*, 21s.
—— *Tent Life in Tiger Land*, with coloured plates, 18s.

IRVING, W., *Little Britain*, 10s. 6d. and 6s.
—— *Works*, "Geoffrey Crayon" edit. 27 vols. 16l. 16s.
JACKSON, John, *Handwriting in Relation to Hygiene*, 3d.
—— *New Style Vertical Writing Copy-Books*, Series I. 1—15, 2d. and 1d. each.
—— *New Code Copy-Books*, 25 Nos. 2d. each.
—— *Shorthand of Arithmetic*, Companion to Arithmetics, 1s. 6d.
—— *Theory and Practice of Handwriting*, with diagrams, 5s.
JALKSON, Lewis, *Ten Centuries of European Progress*, new ed., 5s.
JAMES, Croake, *Law and Lawyers*, new edit. 7s. 6d.
JAMES and MOLE'S *French Dictionary*, 3s. 6d. cloth; roan, 5s.
JAMES, *German Dictionary*, 3s. 6d. cloth; roan, 5s.
JANVIER, *Aztec Treasure House* 7s. 6d., See also Low's Standard Books.
*Japan.* See Foreign Countries.
*Japanese Books*, untearable.
1. Rat's Plaint, by Little, 5s.
2. Smith, Children's Japan, 3s. 6d.
3. Bramhall, Nipouese Rhymes, 5s.
4. Princess Splendor, fairy tale. 2s.
JEFFERIES, Richard, *Amaryllis at the Fair*, 7s. 6d.
—— See also Low's Stan. Books.
JEPHSON, A. J. M., *Emin Pasha relief expedition*, 21s.
—— *Stories told in an African Forest*, 8s. 6d.
JOHNSTON, H. H., *The Congo, from its Mouth to Bolobo*, 21s.
JOHNSTON-LAVIS, H. J., *South Italian Volcanoes*, 15s.

JOHNSTONE, D. L., *Land of the Mountain Kingdom*, new edit. 3s. 6d. and 2s. 6d.
JOINVILLE. See Bayard Ser.
JULIEN, F., *Conversational French Reader*, 2s. 6d.
—— *English Student's French Examiner*, 2s.
—— *First Lessons in Conversational French Grammar*, n. ed. 1s.
—— *French at Home and at School*, Book I. accidence, 2s.; key, 3s.
—— *Petites Leçons de Conversation et de Grammaire*, n. ed. 3s.
—— *Petites Leçons*, with phrases, 3s. 6d.
—— *Phrases of Daily Use*, separately, 6d.
KARR, H. W. Seton, *Shores and Alps of Alaska*, 16s.
KAY. See Foreign Countries.
*Keene (C.), Life*, by Layard, 24s.; l.p., 63s. nett; n. ed., 12s. 6d.
KENNEDY, E. B., *Blacks and Bushrangers*, new edit. 5s., 3s. 6d. and 2s. 6d.
KERSHAW, S. W., *Protestants from France in their English Home*, 6s.
*Khedives and Pashas*, 7s. 6d.
KILNER, E. A., *Four Welsh Counties*, 5s.
*King and Commons.* See Cavalier in Bayard Series.
KINGSLEY, R. G., *Children of Westminster Abbey*, 5s.
KINGSTON. See Low's Standard Books.
KIPLING, Rudyard, *Soldiers Three, &c.*, stories, 1s.
—— *Story of the Gadsbys*, new edit. 1s.

KIPLING, RUDYARD, *In Black and White, &c.,* stories, 1s.
—— *Wee Willie Winkie, &c.,* stories, 1s.
—— *Under the Deodars, &c.,* stories, 1s.
—— *Phantom Rickshaw, &c.,* stories, 1s.
\*\*\* The six collections of stories may also be had in 2 vols. 3s. 6d. each, in cloth.
—— *Stories,* Library Edition, 2 vols. 6s. each.
KIRKALDY, W. G., *David Kirkaldy's Mechanical Testing,* 84s.
KNIGHT, E. F., *Cruise of the Falcon,* 7s. 6d.; new edit. 3s. 6d.
KNOX, T. W., *Boy Travellers with H. M. Stanley,* new edit. 5s.
—— *John Boyd's Adventures,* 6s.
KUNHARDT, C. P., *Small Yachts,* new edit. 50s.
—— *Steam Yachts,* 16s.
KWONG, *English Phrases,* 21s.
LABILLIERE, *Federal Britain,* 6s.
LALANNE, *Etching,* 12s. 6d.
LAMB, CHAS., *Essays of Elia,* with designs by C. O. Murray, 6s.
*Landscape Painters of Holland.* See Great Artists.
LANDSEER. See Great Artists.
LANIER, S., *Boy's Froissart,* 7s. 6d.; *King Arthur,* 7s. 6d.; *Percy,* 7s. 6d.
LANSDELL, HENRY, *Through Siberia,* 2 vols., 30s. See also Low's Standard Library.
—— *Russian Central Asia,* 2 vols. 42s.
—— *Through Central Asia,* 12s.
—— *Chinese Central Asia,* 2 vols., fully illustrated, 36s.
LARDEN, W., *School Course on Heat,* 5th ed., entirely revised, 5s.

LAURIE, A. See Low's Stand. Books.
LAWRENCE, SERGEANT, *Autobiography,* 6s.
LAWRENCE. See Romney in Great Artists.
LAYARD, MRS., *West Indies,* 2s. 6d.
—— G.S., *His Golf Madness,* 1s.
—— See also Keene.
LEA, H. C., *Inquisition in the Middle Ages,* 3 vols., 42s.
LEARED, A., *Morocco,* n. ed. 16s.
LEFFINGWELL, W. B., *Shooting,* 18s.
—— *Wild Fowl Shooting,* 10s. 6d.
LEFROY, W., DEAN OF NORWICH. See Preachers of the Age.
*Leo XIII. Life,* 18s.
*Leonardo da Vinci.* See Great Artists.
—— *Literary Works,* by J. P. Richter, 2 vols. 252s.
LIEBER, *Telegraphic Cipher,* 42s. nett.
*Like unto Christ.* See Gentle Life Series.
*Lincoln, Abraham,* true story of a great life, 2 vols., 12s.
LITTLE, ARCH. J., *Yang-tse Gorges,* n. ed., 10s. 6d.
—— See also Japanese Books.
LITTLE, W. J. KNOX-. See Preachers of the Age.
*Little Masters of Germany.* See Great Artists.
LONG, JAMES, *Farmer's Handbook,* 4s. 6d.
LONGFELLOW, *Maidenhood,* with coloured plates, 2s. 6d.; gilt edges, 3s. 6d.
—— *Nuremberg,* photogravure illustrations, 31s. 6d.

LONGFELLOW, *Song of Hiawatha*, illust., 21s.

LOOMIS, E., *Astronomy*, n. ed. 8s. 6d.

LORD, Mrs. FREWEN, *Tales from Westminster Abbey*, 2s. 6d.; new edition, 1s.

LORNE, MARQUIS OF, *Canada and Scotland*, 7s. 6d.

—— See also Prime Ministers.

Louis, St. See Bayard Series.

*Low's French Readers*, edit. by C. F. Clifton, I. 3d., II. 3d., III. 6d.

—— *German Series.* See Goethe, Meissner, Sandars, and Schiller.

—— *London Charities*, annually, 1s. 6d.; sewed, 1s.

——*Illustrated Germ. Primer*, 1s.

—— *Infant Primers*, I. illus. 3d.; II. illus. 6d.

—— *Pocket Encyclopædia*, with plates, 3s. 6d.; roan, 4s. 6d.

—— *Readers*, Edited by John Gill, I., 9d.; II., 10d.; III., 1s.; IV., 1s. 3d.; V., 1s. 4d.; VI, 1s. 6d.

*Low's Stand. Library of Travel* (unless price is stated), vol. 7s. 6d.

Ashe (R. P.) Two Kings of Uganda, 3s. 6d.; also 6s.

Butler, Great Lone Land; also 3s. 6d.

—— Wild North Land.

Knight, Cruise of the *Falcon*, also 3s. 6d.

Lansdell (H). Through Siberia, unabridged, 10s. 6d.

*Low's Stand. Libr.—continued.*

Marshall (W.) Through America.

Schweinfurth's Heart of Africa, 2 vols. 3s. 6d. each.

Spry (W. J. J., R.N.), *Challenger* cruise.

Stanley (H. M.) Coomassie, 3s. 6d.

—— How I Found Livingstone; also 3s. 6d.

—— Through the Dark Continent, 1 vol. illust., 12s. 6d.; also 3s. 6d.

Thomson, Through Masai Land.

*Low's Standard Novels, Library Edition* (except where price is stated), cr. 8vo., 6s.; also popular edition, small post 8vo, 2s. 6d.; paper bds. 2s.

Baker, John Westacott.

—— Mark Tillotson.

Black (William) Adventures in Thule.

—— The Beautiful Wretch.

—— Daughter of Heth.

—— Donald Ross.

—— Green Pastures & Piccadilly.

—— In Far Lochaber.

—— In Silk Attire.

—— Judith Shakespeare.

—— Kilmeny.

—— Lady Silverdale's Sweetheart.

—— Macleod of Dare.

—— Madcap Violet.

—— Maid of Killeena.

—— New Prince Fortunatus.

—— The Penance of John Logan.

—— Princess of Thule.

—— Sabina Zembra.

—— Shandon Bells.

—— Stand Fast, Craig Royston!

—— Strange Adventures of a House Boat.

—— Strange Adventures of a Phaeton.

—— Sunrise.

—— Three Feathers.

—— White Heather.

—— White Wings.

—— Wise Women of Inverness.

—— Wolfenberg.

—— Yolande.

*Low's Stand. Novels—continued.*

Blackmore (R. D.) Alice Lorraine.
—— Christowell.
—— Clara Vaughan.
—— Cradock Nowell.
—— Cripps the Carrier.
—— Erema, or My Father's Sin.
—— Kit and Kitty.
—— Lorna Doone.
—— Mary Anerley.
—— Springhaven.
—— Tommy Upmore.
Bremont, Gentleman Digger.
Brown (Robert) Jack Abbott's Log.
Bynner, Agnes Surriage.
—— Begum's Daughter.
Cable (G. W.) Bonaventure, 5s.
Coleridge (C. R.) English Squire.
Craddock, Despot of Broomsedge.
Croker (Mrs. B. M.) Some One Else.
Cumberland (Stuart) Vasty Deep.
DeLeon, Under the Stars & Crescent.
Edwards (Miss Betham) Half-way.
Eggleston, Juggernaut.
Emerson (P. H.), Son of the Fens.
French Heiress in her own Chateau.
Gilliat, Story of the Dragonnades.
Harkut, The Conspirator.
Hatton, Old House at Sandwich.
—— Three Recruits.
Hoey (Mrs. Cashel) Golden Sorrow.
—— Out of Court.
—— Stern Chase.
Holmes (O. W.), Guardian Angel.
—— Over the Teacups.
Howard (Blanche W.) Open Door.
Hume (Fergus), Fever of Life.
Ingelow (Jean) Don John.
—— John Jerome, 5s.
—— Sarah de Berenger.
Lathrop, Newport, 5s.
Macalpine, A Man's Conscience.
MacDonald (Geo.) Adela Cathcart.
—— Guild Court.
—— Mary Marston.
—— Orts.
—— Stephen Archer, &c.
—— The Vicar's Daughter.
—— Weighed and Wanting.
Macmaster, Our Pleasant Vices.

*Low's Stand. Novels—continued.*

Martin, Even Mine Own Familiar Friend.
Musgrave (Mrs.) Miriam.
Oliphant, Innocent.
Osborn, Spell of Ashtaroth, 5s.
Prince Maskiloff.
Riddell (Mrs.) Alaric Spenceley.
—— Daisies and Buttercups.
—— Senior Partner.
—— Struggle for Fame.
Russell (W. Clark) Betwixt the Forelands.
—— The Emigrant Ship.
—— Frozen Pirate.
—— Jack's Courtship.
—— John Holdsworth.
—— The Lady Maud.
—— The Little Loo.
—— Mrs. Dines' Jewels, 2s. 6d. and 2s. only.
—— My Watch Below.
—— The Ocean Free Lance.
—— A Sailor's Sweetheart.
—— The Sea Queen.
—— A Strange Voyage.
—— Wreck of the *Grosvenor*.
Ryce, Rector of Amesty.
Steuart, Kilgroom.
Stockton (F. R.) Ardis Claverden.
—— Bee-man of Orn, 5s.
—— Dusantes and Mrs. Lecks and Mrs. Aleshine, 1 vol.
—— Hundredth Man.
—— The late Mrs. Null.
Stoker (Bram) Snake's Pass.
Stowe (Mrs.) Dred.
—— Old Town Folk.
—— Poganuc People.
Thomas, House on the Scar.
Thomson (Joseph) Ulu.
Tourgee, Murvale Eastman.
Tytler (S.) Duchess Frances.
Vane, From the Dead.
—— Polish Conspiracy.
Walford (Mrs.), Her Great Idea.
Warner, Little Journey in the World.
Wilcox, Senora Villena.
Woolson (Constance F.) Anne.
—— East Angels.
—— For the Major, 5s
—— Jupiter Lights.

## *Low's Shilling Novels.*

Edwards, Dream of Millions.
Emerson, East Coast Yarns.
—— Signor Lippo.
Evans, Upper Ten.
Forde, Subaltern, &c.
—— Trotter: a Poona Mystery.
Hewitt, Oriel Penhaligon.
Holman, Life in the Navy.
—— Salt Yarns.
Hume (F.), Creature of the Night.
—— Chinese Jar.
Ignotus; Visitors' Book.
Layard, His Golf Madness.
Married by Proxy.
Rux, Roughing it after Gold.
—— Through the Mill.
Vane, Lynn's Court Mystery.
Vesper, Bobby, a Story.

## *Low's Standard Books for Boys,*
with numerous illustrations, 2s. 6d. each; gilt edges, 3s. 6d.

Ainslie, Priceless Orchid.
Biart (Lucien) Young Naturalist.
—— My Rambles in the New World.
Boussenard, Crusoes of Guiana.
—— Gold Seekers, a sequel.
Butler (Col. Sir Wm.) Red Cloud.
Cahun (Leon) Captain Mago.
—— Blue Banner.
Célière, Exploits of the Doctor.
Chaillu (Paul) Equator Wild Life.
Collingwood, Under the Meteor Flag
—— Voyage of the *Aurora*.
Cozzens (S. W.) Marvellous Country.
Dodge (Mrs.) Hans Brinker.
Du Chaillu (Paul) Gorilla Country.
Erckmann-Chatrian, Bros. Rantzau.
Evelyn, Inca Queen.
Fenn (G. Manville) Off to the Wilds.
—— Silver Cañon.
Groves (Percy) Charmouth Grange.
Heldmann (B.) *Leander* Mutiny.
Henty (G. A.) Cornet of Horse.
—— Jack Archer.
—— Winning his Spurs.
Hyne, Sandy Carmichael.
Janvier, Aztec Treasure House.
Jefferies (Richard) Bevis, Story of a Boy.

## *Low's Stand. Books for Boys—continued.*

Johnstone, Mountain Kingdom.
Kennedy, Blacks and Bushrangers.
Kingston (W. H. G.) Ben Burton.
—— Captain Mugford.
—— Dick Cheveley.
—— Heir of Kilfinnan.
—— Snowshoes.
—— Two Supercargoes.
—— With Axe and Rifle.
Laurie (A.) Axel Ebersen.
—— Conquest of the Moon.
—— New York to Brest.
—— Secret of the Magian.
MacGregor (John) *Rob Roy* Canoe.
—— *Rob Roy* in the Baltic.
—— Yawl *Rob Roy*.
Maclean, Maid of the *Golden Age*.
Malan (A. N.) Cobbler of Cornikeranium.
Meunier, Great Hunting Grounds.
Muller, Noble Words and Deeds.
Norway (G.) How Martin Drake found his Father.
Perelaer, The Three Deserters.
Reed (Talbot Baines) Roger Ingleton, Minor.
—— Sir Ludar.
Reid (Mayne) Strange Adventures.
Rousselet (Louis) Drummer-boy.
—— King of the Tigers.
—— Serpent Charmer.
—— Son of the Constable.
Russell (W. Clark) Frozen Pirate.
Stanley, My Kalulu.
Tregance, Louis, in New Guinea.
Verne, Adrift in the Pacific.
—— Purchase of the North Pole.
Winder (F. H.) Lost in Africa.

## *Low's Standard Series of Books*
by popular writers, cloth gilt, 2s.; gilt edges, 2s. 6d. each.

Alcott (L. M.) A Rose in Bloom.
—— An Old-Fashioned Girl.
—— Aunt Jo's Scrap Bag.
—— Eight Cousins, illust.
—— Jack and Jill.
—— Jimmy's Cruise.

*In all Departments of Literature.*

*Low's Stand. Series of Books—continued.*

Alcott (L. M.) Little Men.
—— Little Women & L.Wo.Wedded
—— Lulu's Library, illust.
—— Recollections of Childhood.
—— Shawl Straps.
—— Silver Pitchers.
—— Spinning-Wheel Stories.
—— Under the Lilacs, illust.
—— Work and Beginning Again, ill.
Alden (W. L.) Jimmy Brown, illust.
—— Trying to Find Europe.
Bunyan, Pilgrim's Progress, 2s.
De Witt (Madame) An Only Sister.
Franc (Maud J.), Stories, 2s. 6d. edition, see page 9.
Holm (Saxe) Draxy Miller's Dowry.
Robinson (Phil) Indian Garden.
—— Under the Punkah.
Roe (E. P.) Nature's Serial Story.
Saintine, Picciola.
Samuels, Forecastle to Cabin, illust.
Sandeau (Jules) Seagull Rock.
Stowe (Mrs.) Dred.
—— Ghost in the Mill, &c.
—— My Wife and I.
—— We and our Neighbours.
Tooley (Mrs.) Harriet B. Stowe.
Warner, In the Wilderness.
—— My Summer in a Garden.
Whitney (Mrs.) Leslie Goldthwaite.
—— Faith Gartney's Girlhood.
—— The Gayworthys.
—— Hitherto.
—— Real Folks.
—— We Girls.
—— The Other Girls: a Sequel.

\*\*\* *A new illustrated list of books for boys and girls, with portraits of celebrated authors, sent post free on application.*

LOWELL, J. R., *Among my Books*, I. and II., 7s. 6d. each.
—— *Vision of Sir Launfal*, illus. 63s.
LUMMIS, C. F., *Tramp, Ohio to California*, 6s.
—— *Land of Poco Tiempo* (New Mexico), 10s. 6d., illust.

MACDONALD, D., *Oceania*, 6s.
—— GEORGE. See Low's Stand. Novels.
—— SIR JOHN A., *Life*, 16s.
MACGOUN, *Commercial Correspondence*, 5s.
MACGREGOR, J., *Rob Roy in the Baltic*, n. ed. 3s. 6d. and 2s. 6d.
—— *Rob Roy Canoe*, new edit., 3s. 6d. and 2s. 6d.
—— *Yawl Rob Roy*, new edit., 3s. 6d. and 2s. 6d.
MACKENNA, *Brave Men in Action*, 10s. 6d.
MACKENZIE, SIR MORELL, *Fatal Illness of Frederick the Noble*, 2s. 6d.
—— *Essays*, 7s. 6d.
MACKINNON and SHADBOLT, *S. African Campaign*, 50s.
MACLAREN, A. See Preachers.
MACLEAN, H. E. See Low's Standard Books.
MACMASTER. See Low's Standard Novels.
MACMULLEN, JOHN MERCER, *History of Canada*, 3rd ed., 2 vols., 25s.
MACMURDO, E., *History of Portugal*, 21s.; II. 21s.; III. 21s.
MAEL, PIERRE, *Under the Sea to the North Pole*, 5s.
MAHAN, CAPT. A. T., *Admiral Farragut*, 6s.
—— *Influence of Sea Power on the French Revolution*, 2 vols. (British naval history), 30s.
—— *Sea Power in History*, 18s.
MAIN, MRS., *My Home in the Alps*, 3s. 6d.
—— See also Burnaby, Mrs.
MALAN. See Low's Stand. Books
—— C. F. DE M., *Eric and Connie's Cruise*, 5s.

*Manchester Library, Reprints of Classics* at nett prices, por vol., 6d.; sewed, 3d.
\*\*\* List on application.

*Man's Thoughts.* See Gentle Life Series.

MANLEY, *Notes on Fish and Fishing.* 6s.

MANTEGNA and FRANCIA. See Great Artists.

MARBURY, *Favourite Flies,* with coloured plates, &c., 24s. nett.

MARCH, F. A., *Comparative Anglo-Saxon Grammar,* 12s.

—— *Anglo-Saxon Reader,* 7s. 6d.

MARKHAM, ADM., *Naval Career during the old war,* 14s.

—— CLEMENTS R., *Peru.* See For. Countries.

—— *War Between Peru and Chili,* 10s. 6d.

MARSH, A. E. W., *Holiday in Madeira,* 5s.

MARSH, G. P., *Lectures on the English Language,* 18s.

—— *Origin and History of the English Language,* 18s.

MARSHALL, W. G., *Through America,* new edit. 7s. 6d.

MARSTON, E., *How Stanley wrote "In Darkest Africa,"* 1s.

—— See also Amateur Angler, Frank's Ranche, and Fresh Woods.

MARSTON, WESTLAND, *Eminent Recent Actors,* n. ed., 6s.

MARTIN, J. W., *Float Fishing and Spinning,* new edit. 2s.

MATHESON, ANNIE, *Love's Music, and other lyrics,* 3s. 6d.

MATTHEWS, J. W., *Incwadi Yami, Twenty Years in S. Africa,* 14s.

MAUCHLINE, ROBERT, *Mine Foreman's Handbook,* 21s.

MAURY, M. F., *Life,* 12s. 6d.

MAURY, M. F., *Physical Geography and Meteorology of the Sea,* new ed. 6s.

MEISSNER, A. L., *Children's Own German Book* (Low's Series), 1s. 6d.

—— *First German Reader* (Low's Series), 1s. 6d.

—— *Second German Reader* (Low's Series), 1s. 6d.

MEISSONIER. See Great Artists.

MELBOURNE, LORD. See Prime Ministers.

MELIO, G. L., *Swedish Drill,* 1s. 6d.

*Member for Wrottenborough,* 3s. 6d.

*Men of Achievement,* 8s. 6d. each.
Noah Brooks, *Statesmen.*
Gen. A. W. Greeley, *Explorers.*
Philip G. Hubert, *Inventors.*
W. O. Stoddard, *Men of Business.*

MENDELSSOHN. *Family,* 1729-1847, Letters and Journals, new edit., 2 vols., 30s.

—— See also Great Musicians.

MERIWETHER, LEE, *Mediterranean,* new ed., 6s.

MERRIFIELD, J., *Nautical Astronomy,* 7s. 6d.

MESNEY, W., *Tungking,* 3s. 6d.

*Metal Workers' Recipes and Processes,* by W. T. Brannt, 12s. 6d.

MEUNIER, V. See Low's Standard Books.

*Michelangelo.* See Great Artists.

MIJATOVICH, C., *Constantine,* 7s. 6d.

MILL, JAMES. See English Philosophers.

MILLS, J., *Alternative Chemistry,* answers to the ordinary course, 1s.

—— *Alternative Elementary Chemistry,* 1s. 6d.; answers, 1s.

MILLS, J., *Chemistry for students*, 3s. 6d.

MILNE, J., AND BURTON, *Volcanoes of Japan*, collotypes by Ogawa, part i., 21s. nett.

MILTON'S *Allegro*. See Choice Editions.

MITCHELL, D.G.(Ik. Marvel) *English Lands, Letters and Kings*, 2 vols. 6s. each.

—— *Writings*, new edit. per vol. 5s.

MITFORD, J., *Letters*, 3s. 6d.

——Miss, *Our Village*, illus. 5s.

MODY, Mrs., *German Literature*, outlines, 1s.

MOFFATT, W., *Land and Work*, 5s.

MOINET. See Preachers.

MOLLETT. See Great Artists.

MOLONEY, J. A., *With Captain Stairs to Katanga*, 8s. 6d.

MONKHOUSE. See G. Artists.

*Montaigne's Essays*, revised by J. Hain Friswell, 2s. 6d.

MONTBARD (G.), *Among the Moors*, illust., 16s. ; ed. de Luxe, 63s.

MOORE, J.M., *New Zealand for Emigrant, Invalid, and Tourist*, 5s.

MORLEY, HENRY, *English Literature in the Reign of Victoria*, 2s. 6d.

—— *Five Centuries of English Literature*, 2s.

MORSE, E. S., *Japanese Homes*, new edit. 10s. 6d.

MORTEN, H., *Hospital Life*, 1s.

—— & GETHEN, *Tales of the Children's Ward*, 3s. 6d.

MORTIMER, J., *Chess Player's Pocket-Book*, new edit. 1s.

MOSS, F. J., *Great South Sea, Atolls and Islands*, 8s. 6d.

MOTTI, PIETRO, *Elementary Russian Grammar*, 2s. 6d.

—— *Russian Conversation Grammar*, 5s. ; Key, 2s.

MOULE, H.C.G. See Preachers.

MOXLY, *West India Sanatorium ; Barbados*, 3s. 6d.

MOXON, W., *Pilocereus Senilis*, 3s. 6d.

MOZART. See Gr. Musicians.

MULLER, E. See Low's Standard Books.

MULLIN, J.P., *Moulding and Pattern Making*, 12s. 6d.

MULREADY. See Gt. Artists.

MURDOCH, *Ayame San*, a Japanese Romance, with photos. reproduced by Ogawa, 30s. nett.

MURILLO. See Great Artists.

MURPHY, *Beyond the Ice, from Farleigh's Diary*, 3s. 6d.

MUSGRAVE, Mrs. See Low's Standard Novels.

*My Comforter, &c., Religious Poems*, 2s. 6d.

*Napoleon I.* See Bayard Series.

NELSON, WOLFRED, *Panama, the Canal*, &c., 6s.

*Nelson's Words and Deeds*, 3s. 6d.

NETHERCOTE, *Pytchley Hunt*, 8s. 6d.

*New Zealand*, chromos, by Barraud, text by Travers, 168s.

NICHOLS, W. L., *Quantocks*, 5s.; large paper, 10s. 6d.

*Nineteenth Century*, a Monthly Review, 2s. 6d. per No.

NISBET, HUME, *Life and Nature Studies*, illustrated, 6s.

NIVEN, R., *Angler's Lexicon*, 6s.

NORMAN, C. B., *Corsairs of France*, 18s.

NORMAN, J. H., *Monetary Systems of the World*, 10s. 6d.
—— *Ready Reckoner of Foreign and Colonial Exchanges*, 2s. 6d.
NORWAY, 50 photogravures by Paul Lange, text by E. J. Goodman, 52s. 6d.
NOTTAGE, C. G., *In Search of a Climate*, illust. 25s.
*Nuggets of the Gouph*, 3s.
O'BRIEN, *Fifty Years of Concession to Ireland*, vol. i. 16s.; vol. ii. 16s.
OGAWA, *Open-Air Life in Japan*, 15s. nett; *Out of doors Life in Japan*, 12s. nett.
OGDEN, J., *Fly-tying*, 2s. 6d.
*Ohrwalder's Ten Years' Captivity; Mahdi's Camp*, new ed., 6s.
*Orient Line Guide*, new edit. by W. J. Loftie, 2s. 6d.
ORTOLI, *Evening Tales*, done into English by J. C. Harris, 6s.
ORVIS, C. F., *Fly Fishing*, with coloured plates, 12s. 6d.
OSBORN, H. S., *Prospector's Guide*, 8s. 6d.
*Other People's Windows.* See Gentle Life Series.
OTTÉ, *Denmark and Iceland.* See Foreign Countries.
*Our Little Ones in Heaven*, 5s.
*Out of Doors Life in Japan*, Burton's photos., from paintings by Ogawa, 12s. net.
*Out of School at Eton*, 2s. 6d.
OVERBECK. See Great Artists.
OWEN, *Marine Insurance*, 15s.
*Oxford Days*, by an M.A., 2s. 6d.
PAGE, T. N., *Marse Chan*, illust. 6s.
—— *Meh Lady*, a Story of Old Virginian Life, 6s.

PALGRAVE, R. F. D. *Chairman's Handbook*, 10th edit. 2s.
—— *Oliver Cromwell*, 10s. 6d.
PALLISER, Mrs. BURY, *China Collector's Companion*, 5s.
—— *History of Lace*, n. ed. 21s.
PANTON, *Homes of Taste*, 2s. 6d.
PARKE, *Emin Pasha Relief Expedition*, 21s., new ed.
—— T. H., *Health in Africa*, 5s.
PARKER, E. H., *Chinese Account of the Opium War*, 1s. 6d.
PARKS, LEIGHTON, *Winning of the Soul, &c.*, sermons, 3s. 6d.
*Parliamentary Pictures and Personalities* (from the *Graphic*), illust., 5s.; ed. de luxo, 21s. nett.
PARSONS, J., *Principles of Partnership*, 31s. 6d.
—— T. P., *Marine Insurance and General Average*, 2 vols. 63s.
PEACH, *Annals of Swainswick*, near Bath, 10s. 6d.
Peel. See Prime Ministers.
PELLESCHI, G., *Gran Chaco of the Argentine Republic*, 8s. 6d.
PEMBERTON, C., *Tyrol*, 1s. 4d.
PENNELL, *Fishing Tackle*, 2s.
—— *Sporting Fish*, 15s. & 30s.
*Penny Postage Jubilee*, 1s.
Peru. See Foreign Countries.
PHELPS, E. S., *Struggle for Immortality*, 5s.
—— SAMUEL, *Life*, by W. M. Phelps & Forbes-Robertson, 12s.
PHILBRICK, F. A., AND WESTOBY, *Post and Telegraph Stamps*, 10s. 6d.
PHILLIMORE, C. M., *Italian Literature*, new. edit. 3s. 6d.
—— See also Gt. Artists, *Fra An.*
PHILLIPS, L. P., *Dictionary of Biographical Reference*, n.e. 25s.
—— W., *Law of Insurance*, 2 vols. 73s. 6d.

PHILPOT, H. J., *Diabetes*, 5s.
—— *Diet Tables*, 1s. each.
*Playtime Library*, 2s. 6d. each.
Charles, Where is Fairy Land?
Humphreys, Little Britons.
Huntingdon, Squire's Nieces.
*Pleasant History of Reynard the Fox*, trans. by T. Roscoe, illus. 7s. 6d.
PLUNKETT (solid geometry) *Orthographic Projection*, 2s. 6d.
POE, by E. C. Stedman, 3s. 6d.
—— *Raven*, ill. by G. Doré, 63s.
*Poems of the Inner Life*, 5s.
*Poetry of Nature.* See Choice Editions.
*Poetry of the Anti-Jacobin*, 7s. 6d. large paper, 21s.
PORCHER, A., *Juvenile French Plays*, with Notes, 1s.
PORTER, Noah, *Memoir*, 8s. 6d.
*Portraits of Racehorses*, 4 vols. 126s.
POSSELT, *Structure of Fibres, Yarns and Fabrics*, 63s.
—— *Textile Design*, illust. 28s.
POYNTER. See Illustrated Text Books.
*Preachers of the Age*, 3s. 6d. ea.
Living Theology, by His Grace the Archbishop of Canterbury.
The Conquering Christ, by Rev. A. Maclaren.
Verbum Crucis, by the Bishop of Derry.
Ethical Christianity, by Hugh P. Hughes.
Knowledge of God, by the Bishop of Wakefield.
Light and Peace, by H. R. Reynolds.
Journey of Life, by W. J. Knox-Little.
Messages to the Multitude, by C. H. Spurgeon.
Christ is All, by H. C. G. Moule, M.A.
Plain Words on Great Themes, by J. O. Dykes.

*Preachers of the Age*—cont.
Children of God, by E. A. Stuart.
Christ in the Centuries, by A. M. Fairbairn.
*Agoniæ Christi*, by Dr. Lefroy.
The Transfigured Sackcloth, by W. L. Watkinson.
The Gospel of Work, by the Bishop of Winchester.
Vision and Duty, by C. A. Berry.
The Burning Bush; Sermons, by the Bishop of Ripon.
Good Cheer of Jesus Christ, by C. Moinet, M.A.
A Cup of Cold Water, by J. Morlais Jones.
The Religion of the Son of Man, by E. J. Gough, M.A.
PRICE, *Arctic Ocean to Yellow Sea*, illust., new ed., 7s. 6d.
*Prime Ministers*, a series of political biographies, edited by Stuart J. Reid, 3s. 6d. each.
Earl of Beaconsfield, by J. Anthony Froude.
Viscount Melbourne, by Henry Dunckley ("*Verax*").
Sir Robert Peel, by Justin McCarthy.
Viscount Palmerston, by the Marquis of Lorne.
Earl Russell, by Stuart J. Reid.
Right Hon. W. E. Gladstone, by G. W. E. Russell.
Earl of Aberdeen, by Sir Arthur Gordon.
Marquis of Salisbury, by H. D. Traill.
Earl of Derby, by G. Saintsbury.
\*<sub>\*</sub>\* *An edition, limited to 250 copies, is issued on hand-made paper, medium 8vo, half vellum, cloth sides, gilt top, 9 vols. 4l. 4s. nett.*
*Prince Maskiloff.* See Low's Standard Novels.
*Prince of Nursery Playmates*, new edit. 2s. 6d.
PRITT, T. N., *North Country Flies*, coloured plates, 10s. 6d.
*Reynolds.* See Great Artists.

*Purcell.* See Great Musicians.
PYLE, HOWARD, *Robin Hood,* 10s. 6d.
QUILTER, HARRY, *Giotto, Life, &c.* 15s.
—— See also Great Artists.
RAMBAUD, *History of Russia,* new edit., 3 vols. 21s.
RAPHAEL. See Great Artists.
READ, OPIE, *Emmett Bonlore,* 6s.
REDFORD, *Sculpture.* See Illustrated Text-books.
REDGRAVE, *Century of English Painters,* new ed., 7s. 6d.
REED, SIR E. J., *Modern Ships of War,* 10s. 6d.
—— T. B. See Low's St. Bks.
REID, MAYNE, CAPTAIN. See Low's Standard Books.
—— STUART J. See Prime Min.
*Remarkable Bindings in British Museum,* 168s.; 94s. 6d.; 73s. 6d. and 63s.
REMBRANDT. See Gr. Artists.
REYNOLDS. See Gr. Artists.
—— HENRY R. See Preachers.
RICHARDS, J. W., *Aluminium,* new edit. 21s.
RICHTER, *Italian Art in the National Gallery,* 42s.
—— See also Great Artists.
RIDDELL, MRS. J. H. See Low's Standard Novels.
RIFFAULT, *Colours for Painting,* 31s. 6d.
RIPON, BP. OF. See Preachers.
RIVIÈRE, J., *Recollections,* 3s. 6d.
ROBERTS. See For. Countries.
—— W., *English Bookselling,* earlier history, 7s. 6d.; n. ed. 3s. 6d.
ROBERTSON, AL., *Fra Paolo Sarpi, the Greatest of the Venetians,* 6s.
—— *Count Campello,* 5s.

ROBIDA, A., *Toilette,* coloured plates, 7s. 6d.; new ed. 3s. 6d.
ROBINSON, PHIL., *Noah's Ark,* n. ed. 3s. 6d.
—— *Sinners & Saints,* 10s. 6d.; new ed. 3s. 6d.
—— See also Low's Stan. Ser.
—— SERJ., *Wealth and its Sources,* 5s.
—— J. R., *Princely Chandos,* illust., 12s. 6d.
—— *Last Earls of Barrymore,* 12s. 6d.
—— *"Romeo" Coates,* 7s. 6d.
ROCHEFOUCAULD. See Bayard Series.
ROCKSTRO, *History of Music,* new ed. 14s.
RODRIGUES, *Panama Can.,* 5s.
ROE, E. P. See Low's St. Ser.
ROGERS, S. See Choice Eds.
ROLFE, *Pompeii,* n. ed., 7s. 6d.
—— H. L., *Fish Pictures,* 15s.
ROMNEY. See Great Artists.
ROOPER, G., *Thames and Tweed.*
ROSE, J., *Mechanical Drawing Self-Taught,* 16s.
—— *Key to Engines,* 8s. 6d.
—— *Practical Machinist,* new ed. 12s. 6d.
—— *Steam Engines,* 31s. 6d.
—— *Steam Boilers,* 12s. 6d.
*Rose Library.* Per vol. 1s., unless the price is given.
Alcott (L. M.) Eight Cousins, 2s.
—— Jack and Jill, 2s.
—— Jimmy's cruise in the Pinafore, 2s.; cloth, 3s. 6d.
—— Little Women.
—— Little Women Wedded; Nos. 4 and 5 in 1 vol. cloth, 3s. 6d.
—— Little Men, 2s.; cl. gt., 3s. 6d.
—— Old-fashioned Girls, 2s.; cloth, 3s. 6d.
—— Rose in Bloom, 2s.; cl. 3s. 6d.

*In all Departments of Literature.* 25

*Rose Library—Continued.*
Alcott (L. M.) Silver Pitchers.
—— Under the Lilacs, 2s.; cl.3s.6d.
—— Work, 2 vols. in 1, cloth, 3s.6d.
Stowe (Mrs.) Pearl of Orr's Island.
—— Minister's Wooing.
—— We and Our Neighbours, 2s.
—— My Wife and I, 2s.
Dodge (Mrs.) Hans Brinker, 1s.; cloth, 5s.; 3s. 6d.; 2s. 6d.
Holmes, Guardian Angel, cloth, 2s.
Stowe (Mrs.) Dred,2s.; cl. gt.,3s 6d.
Carleton (W.) City Ballads, 2 vols. in 1, cloth gilt, 2s. 6d.
—— Legends, 2 vols. in 1, cloth gilt, 2s. 6d.
—— Farm Ballads, 6d. and 9d.; 3 vols. in 1, cloth gilt, 3s. 6d.
—— Farm Festivals, 3 vols. in 1, cloth gilt, 3s. 6d.
—— Farm Legends, 3 vols. in 1, cloth gilt, 3s. 6d.
Biart, Bernagius' Clients, 2 vols.
Howells, Undiscovered Country.
Clay (C. M.) Baby Rue.
—— Story of Helen Troy.
Whitney, Hitherto, 2 vols. 3s. 6d.
Fawcett (E.) Gentleman of Leisure.
Butler, Nothing to Wear.
ROSSETTI. See Wood.
ROSSINI, &c. See Great Mus.
*Rothschilds*, by J. Reeves,7s. 6d.
*Roughing it after Gold,* by Rux, new edit. 1s.
ROUSSELET. See Low's Standard Books.
*Royal Naval Exhibition,* illus.1s.
RUBENS. See Great Artists.
RUSSELL, G.W. E.,*Gladstone.* See Prime Ministers.
—— H., *Ruin of Soudan,* 21s.
—— W. CLARK, *Mrs. Dines' Jewels,* boards, 2s.
—— *Nelson's Words and Deeds,* 3s. 6d.
—— *Sailor's Language,* 3s. 6d.
—— See also Low's Standard Novels.

RUSSELL, W. HOWARD,*Prince of Wales' Tour,* ill. 52s. 6d. and 84s.
*Russia.* See Foreign Countries.
*Russia's March towards India,* by an Indian Officer, 2 vols., 16s.
*Saints and their Symbols,* 3s. 6d.
SAINTSBURY, G., *Earl of Derby.* See Prime Ministers.
SAINTINE. See Low's Stan. Series.
SALISBURY, LORD. See Prime Ministers.
SAMUELS. See Low's Standard Series.
SAMUELSON, JAMES, *Greece, her Condition and Progress*, 3s.6d.
SANBORN, KATE, *A Truthful Woman in Southern California,* 3s. 6d.
SANDARS,*German Primer,* 1s.
SANDEAU. See Low's Stand. Series.
SANDLANDS, *How to Develop Vocal Power,* 1s.
SAUER, *European Commerce,* 5s.
—— *Italian Grammar* (Key, 2s.), 5s.
—— *Spanish Dialogues,* 2s. 6d.
—— *Spanish Grammar* (Key, 2s.), 5s.
—— *Spanish Reader,* new edit. 3s. 6d.
*Scenes from Open-Air Life in Japan,* photo plates by Ogawa, text by Murdoch, 15s. net.
SCHAACK, *Anarchy,* 16s.
SCHERER, *Essays in English Literature,* by G. Saintsbury, 6s.
SCHILLER'S *Prosa,* 2s. 6d.
SCHUBERT. See Great Mus.
SCHUMANN. See Great Mus.
SCHWAB, *Age of the Horse* ascertained by the teeth, 2s. 6d.

SCHWEINFURTH. See Low's Standard Library.
*Scientific Education of Dogs*, 6s.
SCOTT, LEADER, *Renaissance of Art in Italy*, 31s. 6d.
—— See also Great Artists and Illust. Text Books.
—— SIR GILBERT, *Autobiography*, 18s.
—— W. B. See Great Artists.
*Scribner's Magazine*, monthly, 1s.; half-yearly volumes, 8s. 6d.
*Sea Stories.* See Russell in Low's Standard Novels.
SEVERN, JOSEPH, *Life, Letters, and Friendships*, by Sharp, 21s.
*Shadow of the Rock*, 2s. 6d.
SHAFTESBURY. See English Philosophers.
SHAKESPEARE, ed. by R. G. White, 3 vols. 36s.; l. paper, 63s.
—— *Annals; Life & Work*, 2s.
—— *Hamlet*, 1603, also 1604, 7s. 6d.
—— *Heroines*, by living painters, 105s.; artists' proofs, 630s.
—— *Macbeth*, with etchings, 105s. and 52s. 6d.
—— *Songs and Sonnets*. See Choice Editions.
SHEPHERD, *British School of Painting*, 2nd edit. 5s.; also sewed, 1s.
SHOCK, W. H. *Steam Boilers*, 73s. 6d.
*Silent Hour.* See Gentle Life Series.
SIDNEY, SIR PHILIP, *Arcadia*, new ed., 6s.
SIMSON, *Ecuador and the Putumayor River*, 8s. 6d.
SKOTTOWE, *Hanoverian Kings*, new edit. 3s. 6d.
SLOANE, T. O., *Home Experiments in Science*, 6s.

SLOANE, W. M., *French War and the Revolution*, 7s. 6d.
SMITH, CHARLES W., *Theories and Remedies for Depression in Trade, &c.*, 2s.
—— *Commercial Gambling the Cause of Depression*, 3s. 6d.
—— G., *Assyria*, 18s.
—— *Chaldean Account of Genesis*, new edit. by Sayce, 18s.
—— GERARD. See Illustrated Text Books.
—— MRS. See Japanese.
—— T. ASSHETON, *Reminiscences* by Sir J. E. Wilmot, n. ed., 2s. 6d. and 2s.
—— T. ROGER. See Illustrated Text Books.
—— W. A., *Shepherd Smith, the Universalist*, 8s. 6d.
—— HAMILTON, and LEGROS' *French Dictionary*, 2 vols. 16s., 21s., and 22s.
*Socrates.* See Bayard Series.
SNOWDEN (J. KEIGHLEY) *Tales of the Yorkshire Wolds*, 3s. 6d.
SOMERSET, *Our Village Life*, with coloured plates, 5s.
*Spain.* See Foreign Countries.
SPIERS, *French Dictionary*, new ed., 2 vols. 18s., half bound, 21s.
SPRY. See Low's Standard Library.
SPURGEON, C. H. See Preachers.
STANLEY, H. M., *Congo*, 2 vols. 42s. new ed., 2 vols., 21s.
—— *Emin's Rescue*, 1s.
—— *In Darkest Africa*, 2 vols., 42s.; new edit. 1 vol. 10s. 6d.
—— *My Dark Companions and their Strange Stories*, illus. 7s. 6d.
—— See also Low's Standard Library and Low's Stand. Books.

START, *Exercises in Mensuration*, 8d.

STEPHENS. See Great Artists.

STERNE. See Bayard Series.

STERRY, J. ASHBY, *Cucumber Chronicles*, 5s.

STEUART, J. A., *Letters to Living Authors*, new edit. 2s. 6d.; édit. de luxe, 10s. 6d.

—— See also Low's Standard Novels.

STEVENI (N. B.). *Through Famine-Stricken Russia*, 3s. 6d.

STEVENS, J. W., *Leather Manufacture*, illust. 18s.

—— T., *Around the World on a Bicycle*, 16s.; part II. 16s.

STEWART, DUGALD, *Outlines of Moral Philosophy*, 3s. 6d.

STOCKTON, F. R., *Ardis Claverden*, 6s.

—— *Clocks of Rondaine, and other Stories*, 7s. 6d.

—— *Mrs. Lecks*, 1s.

—— *The Dusantes*, a sequel to Mrs. Lecks, 1s.

—— *Personally Conducted*, (tour in Europe), illust. 7s. 6d.

—— *Rudder Grangers Abroad*, 2s. 6d.

—— *Schooner Merry Chanter*, 2s. 6d. and 1s.

—— *Squirrel Inn*, illust. 6s.

—— *Story of Viteau*, 5s., 3s.6d.

—— *Three Burglars*, 2s. & 1s.

—— See also Low's Standard Novels.

STOKER, BRAM, *Under the Sunset*, Christmas Stories, 6s.

STORER, F. H., *Agriculture and Chemistry*, 2 vols., 25s.

*Stories from Scribner*, illust., 6 vols., transparent wrapper. 1s. 6d. each; cloth, top gilt, 2s. each.
  I. Of New York.
  II. Of the Railway.
  III. Of the South.
  IV. Of the Sea.
  VI. Of Italy.
  V. Of the Army.

STOWE, MRS., *Flowers and Fruit from Her Writings*, 3s. 6d.

—— *Life . . . her own Words . . . Letters, &c.*, 15s.

—— *Life*, for boys and girls, by S. A. Tooley, 5s., 2s. 6d. and 2s.

—— *Little Foxes*, cheap edit. 1s.; also 4s. 6d.

—— *Minister's Wooing*, 1s.

—— *Pearl of Orr's Island*, 3s. 6d. and 1s.

—— *Uncle Tom's Cabin*, with 126 new illust. 2 vols. 16s.

—— See also Low's Standard Novels and Low's Standard Series.

STRACHAN, J., *New Guinea, Explorations*, 12s.

STRANAHAN, *French Painting*, 21s.

STRICKLAND, F., *Engadine*, new edit. 5s.

STRONGE, S. E., & EAGAR, *English Grammar*, 3s.

STUART, E. A. See Preachers.

—— ESMÉ, *Claudex's Island*, 6s.

STUTFIELD, *El Maghreb*, 8s. 6d.

SUMNER, C., *Memoir*, vols. iii., iv., 36s.

*Sweden and Norway*. See Foreign Countries.

*Sylvanus Redivivus*, 10s. 6d.; new ed., 3s. 6d.

SZCZEPANSKI, *Technical Literature*, a directory, 2s.

TAINE, H. A., *Origines*, I. Ancient Regime and French Revolution, 3 vols., 16s. ea.; Modern, I. and II., 16s. ea.

TAYLER, J., *Beyond the Bustle*, 6s.

TAYLOR, Hannis, *English Constitution*, 18s.

—— Mrs. Bayard, *Letters to a Young Housekeeper*, 5s.

—— R. L., *Analysis Tables*, 1s.

—— *Chemistry*, n. ed., 2s.

—— *Students' Chemistry*, 5s.

—— and S. PARRISH, *Chemical Problems, with Solutions*, 2s. 6d.

*Techno-Chemical Receipt Book*, by Brannt and Wahl, 10s. 6d.

TENNYSON. See Choice Eds.

THANET, *Stories of a Western Town* (United States), 6s.

THAUSING, *Malt & Beer*, 45s.

THEAKSTON, *British Angling Flies*, illust., 5s.

*Thomas à Kempis Birthday-Book*, 3s. 6d.

—— *Daily Text-Book*, 2s. 6d.

—— See also Gentle Life Series.

THOMAS, Bertha, *House on the Scar, Tale of South Devon*, 6s.

THOMSON, Joseph. See Low's Stan. Lib. and Low's Stan. Novs.

—— W., *Algebra*, 5s.; without Answers, 4s. 6d.; Key, 1s. 6d.

THORNTON, W. Pugin, *Heads, and what they tell us*, 1s.

THORODSEN, J P., *Lad and Lass*, 6s.

TILESTON, Mary W., *Daily Strength*, 5s. and 3s. 6d.

TINTORETTO. See Gr. Art.

TITIAN. See Great Artists.

TODD, Alphaeus, *Parliamentary Government in England*, 2 vols., 15s.

TOLSTOI, A. K., *The Terrible Czar, a Romance of the time of Ivan the Terrible*, new ed. 6s.

TOMPKINS, *Through David's Realm*, illust. by author., n. ed., 5s.

TOURGEE. See Low's Standard Novels.

TRACY, A., *Rambles Through Japan without a Guide*, 6s.

TRAILL. See Prime Ministers.

TURNER, J. M. W. See Gr. Artists.

TYACKE, Mrs., *How I shot my Bears*, illust., 7s. 6d.

TYTLER, Sarah. See Low's Standard Novels.

UPTON, H., *Dairy Farming*, 2s.

*Valley Council*, by P. Clarke, 6s.

VANDYCK and HALS. See Great Artists.

VAN DYKE, J. C., *Art for Art's Sake*, 7s. 6d.

VANE, Denzil, *Lynn's Court Mystery*, 1s.

—— See also Low's St. Nov.

Vane, *Young Sir Harry*, 18s.

VAN HARE, *Showman's Life, Fifty Years*, new ed., 2s. 6d.

VELAZQUEZ. See Gr. Artists.
—— and MURILLO, by C. B. Curtis, with etchings, 31s. 6d.; large paper, 63s.
VERNE, J., *Works by.* See last page but one.
*Vernet and Delaroche.* See Great Artists.
VERSCHUUR, G., *At the Antipodes,* 7s. 6d.
VINCENT, Mrs. Howard, 40,000 *Miles over Land and Water,* 2 vols. 21s.; also 3s. 6d.
—— *Newfoundland to Cochin China,* new ed. 3s. 6d.
*Visitors' Book in a Swiss Hotel,* 1s.
WAGNER. See Gr. Musicians.
WAHNSCHAFFE, *Scientific Examination of Soil,* by Brannt, 8s. 6d.
WALERY, *Our Celebrities,* vol. II. part i., 30s.
WALFORD, Mrs. L. B. See Low's Standard Novels.
WALL, *Tombs of the Kings of England,* 21s.
WALLACE, L., *Ben Hur,* 2s.
WALLER, *Silver Sockets,* 6s.
WALTON, Iz., *Angler,* Lea and Dove edit. by R. B. Marston, with photos., 210s. and 105s.
—— T. H., *Coal-mining,* 25s.
WARBURTON, Col., *Race-horse, How to Buy, &c.,* 6s.
WARDROP, Ol., *Kingdom of Georgia,* 14s.
WARNER, C. D. See Low's Stand. Novels and Low's Stand. Series.
WARREN, W. F., *Paradise Found,* illust. 12s. 6d.

WATKINSON. See Preachers.
WATTEAU. See Great Artists.
WEBER. See Great Musicians.
WELLINGTON. See Bayard Series.
WELLS, H. P., *Salmon Fisherman,* 6s.
WELLS, H. P., *Fly-rods and Tackle,* 10s. 6d.
WENZEL, *Chemical Products of the German Empire,* 25s.
*West Indies.* See Foreign Countries.
WESTGARTH, *Australasian Progress,* 12s.
WESTOBY, *Postage Stamps,* 5s.
WHITE, R. Grant, *England Without and Within,* new edit. 10s. 6d.
—— *Every-day English,* 10s. 6d.
—— *Studies in Shakespeare,* 10s. 6d.
—— *Words and their Uses,* new edit. 5s.
—— W., *Our English Homer, Shakespeare and his Plays,* 6s.
WHITNEY, Mrs. See Low's Standard Series.
WHITTIER, *St. Gregory's Guest,* 5s.
—— *Text and Verse for Every Day in the Year,* selections, 1s. 6d.
WILCOX, Marrion. See Low's Standard Novels.
WILKIE. See Great Artists.
WILLS, *Persia as it is,* 8s. 6d.
WILSON, *Health for the People,* 7s. 6d.

WINCHESTER, Bishop of. See Preachers of the Age.

WINDER, *Lost in Africa.* See Low's Standard Books.

WINGATE. See Ohrwalder.

WINSOR, J., *Columbus*, 21s.

—— *Cartier to Frontenac,* A Study of Geographical Discovery in the Interior of North America, 1534—1700, with reproductions of old maps, 15s.

—— *History of America,* 8 vols. per vol. 30s. and 63s.

WITTHAUS, *Chemistry*, 16s.

*Woman's Mission, Congress Papers,* edited by the Baroness Burdett-Coutts, 10s. 6d.

WOOD, Esther, *Dante Gabriel Rossetti and the Preraphaelite Movement,* with illustrations from Rossetti's paintings, 12s. 6d.

—— Sir Evelyn, *Life,* by Williams, 11s.

WOODS, *Sweden and Norway.* See Foreign Countries.

WOOLSEY, *Communism and Socialism,* 7s. 6d.

—— *International Law,* 6th ed. 18s.

—— *Political Science,* 2 v. 30s.

WOOLSON, C. Fenimore. See Low's Standard Novels.

WORDSWORTH. See Choice.

*Wreck of the "Grosvenor,"* 4to, paper cover, 6d.

WRIGHT, H., *Friendship of God,* 6s.

—— T., *Town of Cowper,* 3s. 6d.

WRIGLEY, *Algiers Illustrated,* 100 views in photogravure, 45s.

*Written to Order,* 6s.

YOUNGHUSBAND, Capt. G. J., *On Short Leave to Japan,* illust. 6s.

# BOOKS BY JULES VERNE.

| LARGE CROWN 8vo. WORKS. | Containing 350 to 600 pp. and from 50 to 100 full-page illustrations. || Containing the whole of the text with some illustrations. ||
|---|---|---|---|---|
| | Handsome cloth binding, gilt edges. | Plainer binding, plain edges. | Cloth binding, gilt edges, smaller type. | Limp cloth. |
| | s. d. | s. d. | s. d. | s. d. |
| 20,000 Leagues under the Sea. Parts I. and II. | 10 6 | 5 0 | 3 6 | 2 0 |
| Hector Servadac | 10 6 | 5 0 | 3 6 | 2 0 |
| The Fur Country | 10 6 | 5 0 | 3 6 | 2 0 |
| The Earth to the Moon and a Trip round it | 10 6 | 5 0 | 2 vols., 2s. ea. | 2 vols., 1s. ea. |
| Michael Strogoff | 10 6 | 5 0 | 3 6 | 2 0 |
| Dick Sands, the Boy Captain | 10 6 | 5 0 | 3 6 | 2 0 |
| Five Weeks in a Balloon | 7 6 | 3 6 | 2 0 | 1 0 |
| Adventures of Three Englishmen and Three Russians | 7 6 | 3 6 | 2 0 | 1 0 |
| Round the World in Eighty Days | 7 6 | 3 6 | 2 0 | 1 0 |
| A Floating City | 7 6 | 3 6 | 2 0 | 1 0 |
| The Blockade Runners | | | 2 0 | 1 0 |
| Dr. Ox's Experiment | — | — | 2 0 | 1 0 |
| A Winter amid the Ice | — | — | 2 0 | 1 0 |
| Survivors of the "Chancellor" | 7 6 | 3 6 | 3 6 | 2 0 |
| Martin Paz | | | 2 0 | 1 0 |
| The Mysterious Island, 3 vols.:— | 23 6 | 10 6 | 6 0 | 3 0 |
|   I. Dropped from the Clouds | 7 6 | 3 6 | 2 0 | 1 0 |
|   II. Abandoned | 7 6 | 3 6 | 2 0 | 1 0 |
|   III. Secret of the Island | 7 6 | 3 6 | 2 0 | 1 0 |
| The Child of the Cavern | 7 6 | 3 6 | 2 0 | 1 0 |
| The Begum's Fortune | 7 6 | 3 6 | 2 0 | 1 0 |
| The Tribulations of a Chinaman | 7 6 | 3 6 | 2 0 | 1 0 |
| The Steam House, 2 vols.:— | | | | |
|   I. Demon of Cawnpore | 7 6 | 3 6 | 2 0 | 1 0 |
|   II. Tigers and Traitors | 7 6 | 3 6 | 2 0 | 1 0 |
| The Giant Raft, 2 vols.:— | | | | |
|   I. 800 Leagues on the Amazon | 7 6 | 3 6 | 2 0 | 1 0 |
|   II. The Cryptogram | 7 6 | 3 6 | 2 0 | 1 0 |
| The Green Ray | 5 0 | 3 6 | 2 0 | 1 0 |
| Godfrey Morgan | 7 6 | 3 6 | 2 0 | 1 0 |
| Kéraban the Inflexible:— | | | | |
|   I. Captain of the "Guidara" | 7 6 | 3 6 | 2 0 | 1 0 |
|   II. Scarpante the Spy | 7 6 | 3 6 | 2 0 | 1 0 |
| The Archipelago on Fire | 7 6 | 3 6 | 2 0 | 1 0 |
| The Vanished Diamond | 7 6 | 3 6 | 2 0 | 1 0 |
| Mathias Sandorf | 10 6 | 5 0 | 3 6 | 2 vols 1 0 each |
| Lottery Ticket | 7 6 | 3 6 | 2 0 | 1 0 |
| The Clipper of the Clouds | 7 6 | 3 6 | 2 0 | 1 0 |
| North against South | 7 6 | 3 6 | — | 2 vols 1 0 each |
| Adrift in the Pacific | 6 0 | 2 6 | | |
| The Flight to France | 7 6 | 3 6 | 1 0 | |
| The Purchase of the North Pole | 6 0 | 2 6 | | |
| A Family without a Name | 6 0 | | | |
| César Cascabel | 6 0 | | | |
| Mistress Branican | 6 0 | | | |
| Castle of the Carpathians | 6 0 | | | |

\*\*\* *Special issue in eight cases of five books each, in a box, 4s. per box.*

CELEBRATED TRAVELS AND TRAVELLERS. 3 vols. 8vo, 600 pp., 100 full-page illustrations, 7s. 6d., gilt edges, 9s. each:—(1) THE EXPLORATION OF THE WORLD. (2) THE GREAT NAVIGATORS OF THE EIGHTEENTH CENTURY. (3) THE GREAT EXPLORERS OF THE NINETEENTH CENTURY.

# SAMPSON LOW, MARSTON & CO.'S PERIODICAL PUBLICATIONS.

### THE NINETEENTH CENTURY.

A Monthly Review. Edited by JAMES KNOWLES. Price Half-a-Crown.

Amongst the Contributors the following representative names may be mentioned: The Right Hon. W. E. Gladstone, Mr. J. A. Froude, Mr. Ruskin, Mr. G. F. Watts, R.A., Earl Grey, the Earl of Derby, Lord Acton, Mr. Herbert Spencer, Mr. Frederick Harrison, Mr. Algernon C. Swinburne, Mr. Leslie Stephen, Professor Huxley, Sir Theodore Martin, Sir Edward Hamley, Professor Goldwin Smith, and Sir Samuel Baker.

### SCRIBNER'S MAGAZINE.

A Superb Illustrated Monthly. Price One Shilling.

Containing Contributions from the pens of many well-known Authors, among whom may be mentioned, Thomas Hardy, J. M. Barrie, Walter Besant, Bret Harte, Henry James, Thomas Bailey Aldrich, Sir Edwin Arnold, Andrew Lang, Sarah Orme Jewett, H. M. Stanley, Robert Louis Stevenson, R. H. Stoddard, Frank R. Stockton.

### THE PUBLISHERS' CIRCULAR

### and Booksellers' Record of British and Foreign Literature.

Weekly. Every Saturday. Price Three-Halfpence. Subscription: Inland, Twelve Months (post free), 8s. 6d.; Countries in the Postal Union, 11s.

### THE FISHING GAZETTE.

A Journal for Anglers. Edited by R. B. MARSTON, Hon. Treas. of the Fly Fishers' Club. Published Weekly, price 2d. Subscription, 10s. 6d. per annum.

The *Gazette* contains every week Twenty folio pages of Original Articles on Angling of every kind. The paper has recently been much enlarged and improved.

"Under the editorship of Mr. R. B. Marston the *Gazette* has attained a high standing."—*Daily News.* "An excellent paper."—*The World.*

### BOYS.

A new High-class Illustrated Journal for our Lads and Young Men. Weekly, One Penny; Monthly, Sixpence; Annual Vol., 7s. 6d.

LONDON: SAMPSON LOW, MARSTON & COMPANY, LIMITED,
ST. DUNSTAN'S HOUSE, FETTER LANE, FLEET STREET E.C.

www.ingramcontent.com/pod-product-compliance
Lightning Source LLC
Chambersburg PA
CBHW030318170426
43202CB00009B/1059